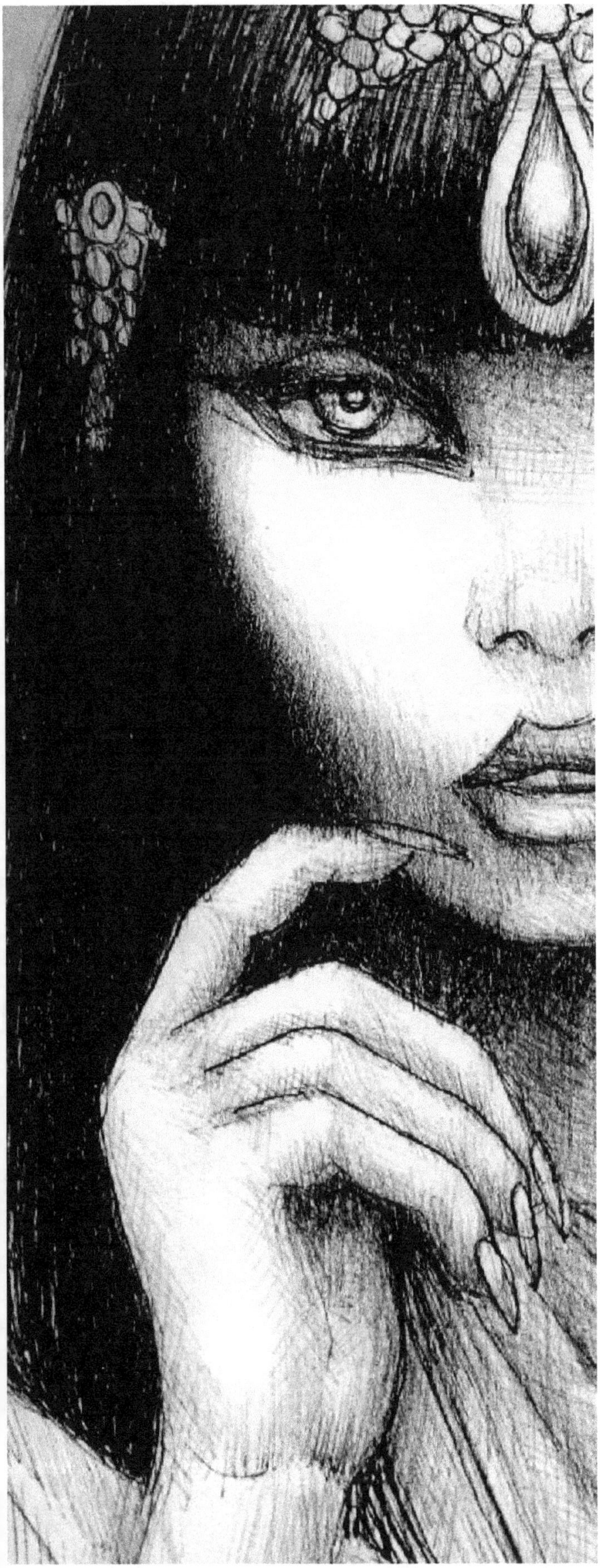

THE LOST ART VOLUME 2

HOW TO DRAW FANTASY FEMALE FACES

BY
FRANK
GRANADOS

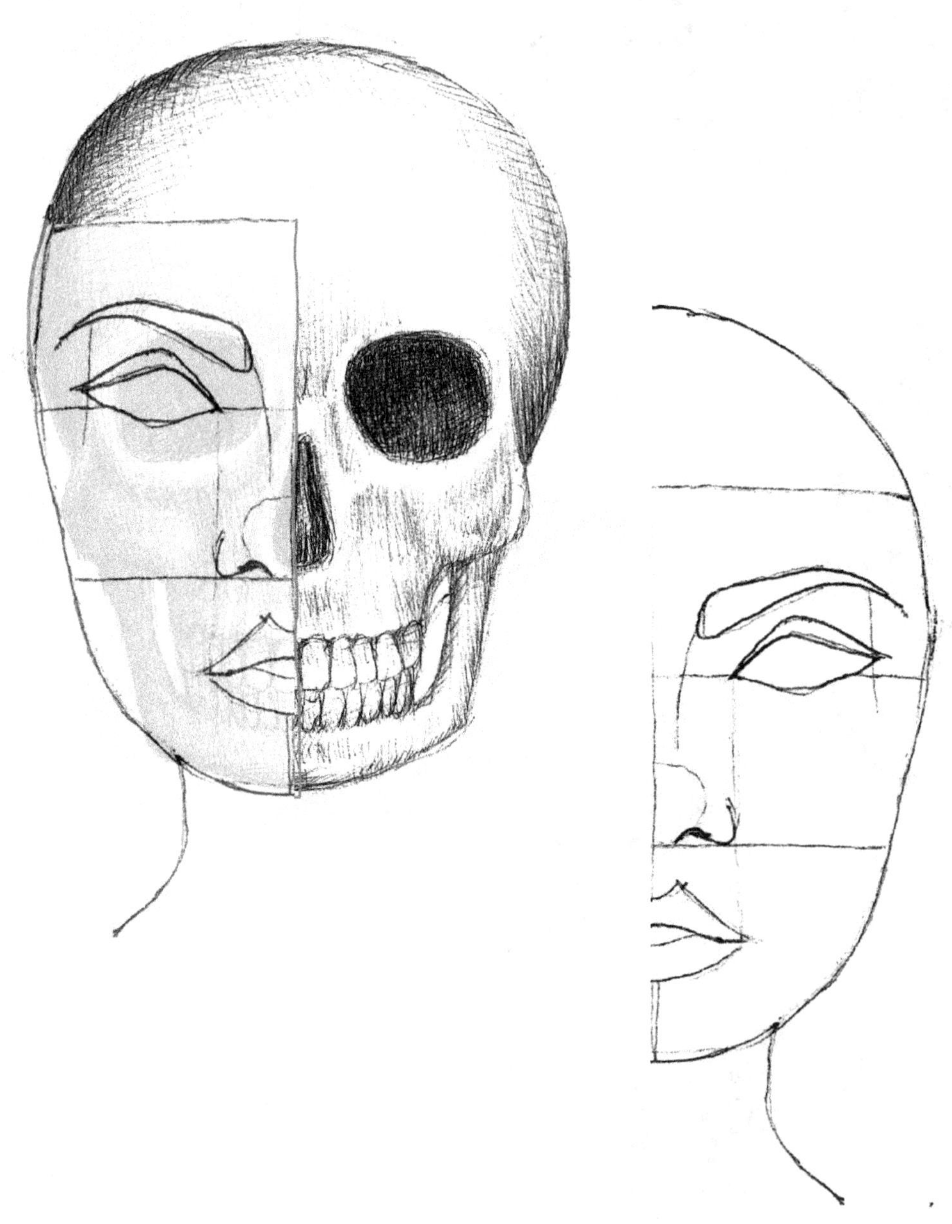

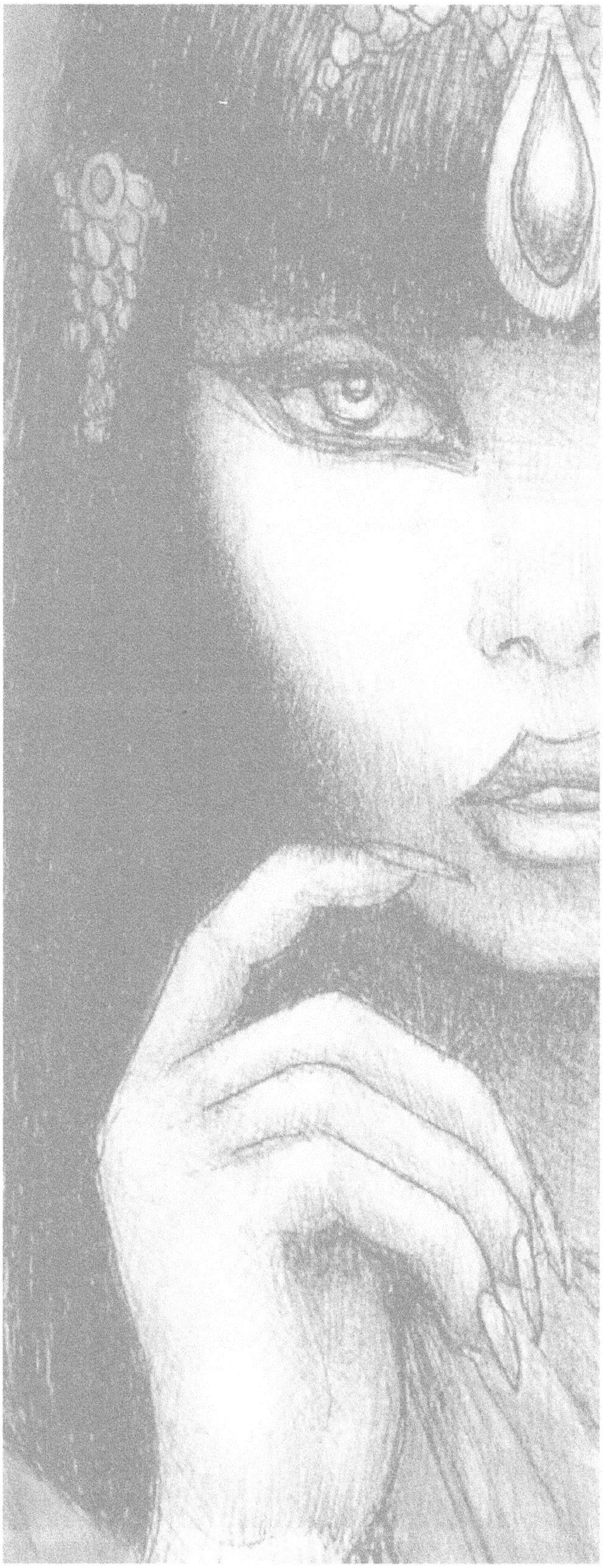

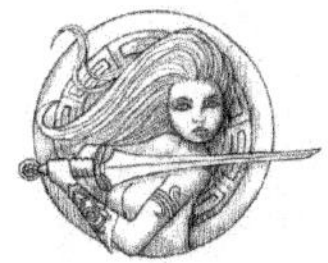

Published by
Phoenician Press ©2013

All drawings and illustrations are the original works of art done exclusively by Frank Granados. Any resemblances or similarities, to persons or characters living or dead, is purely coincidental and not intentional.

The Lost Art: Volume 2
How To Draw Fantasy Female Faces
Authored by Frank Granados

ISBN-13: 978-0615835594
ISBN-10: 0615835597

BISAC: Art / Techniques / Drawing

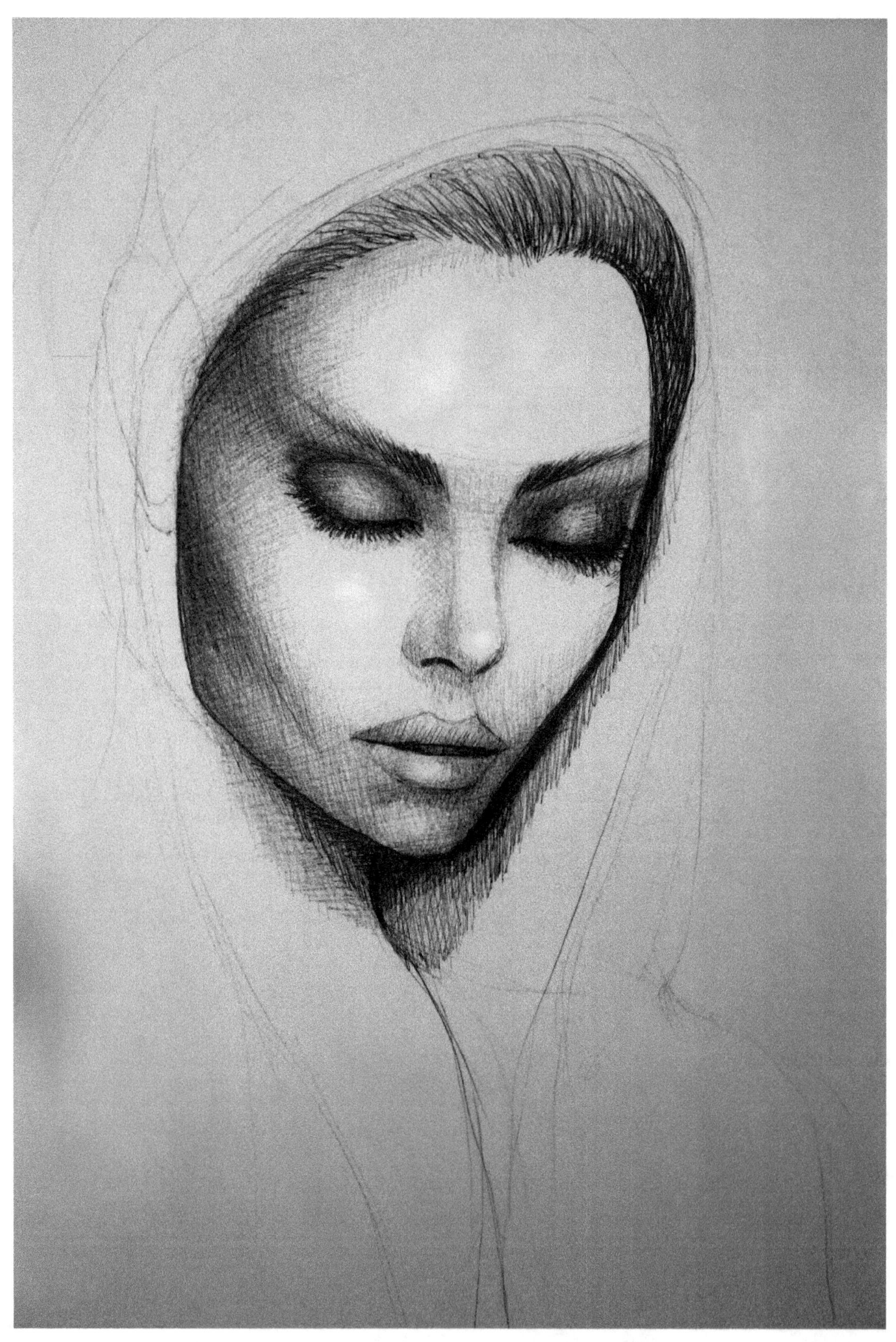

To Delia

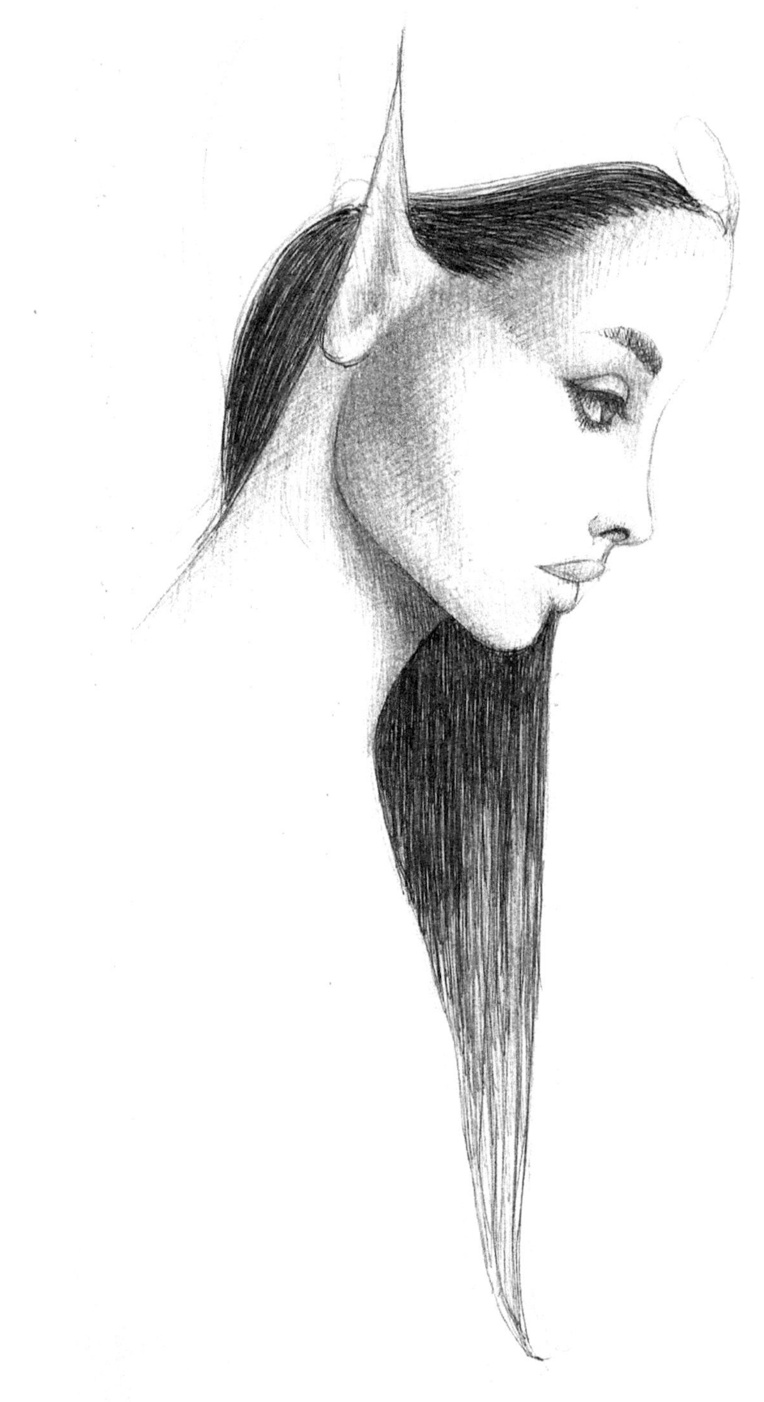

As she sleeps among the skulls, in the ruins of her shattered castle, each night she falls into her sweet book of dreams.
Her soul yearns to escape into the sun.
She can feel the wings behind her as they carry her across the oceans of her soul.
She soars across the heavens, beyond the stars, to an unreachable destination found only in her dreams.
She is terrorized by the reality that she is hunted by a demon.
Trapped inside a nightmare that no living being can escape from.
Trapped and bound by the beast she is the prisoner of your dreams.

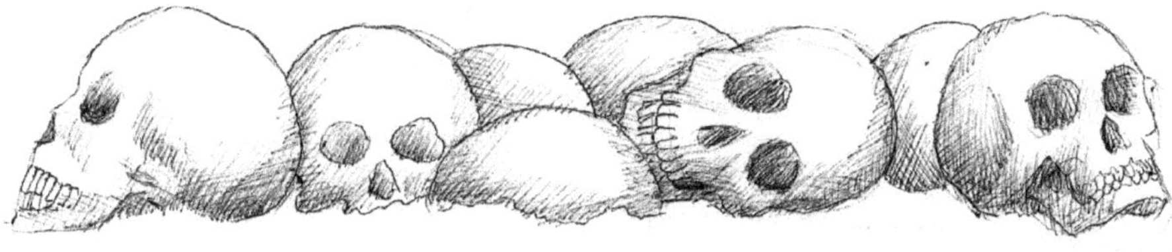

TABLE OF CONTENTS

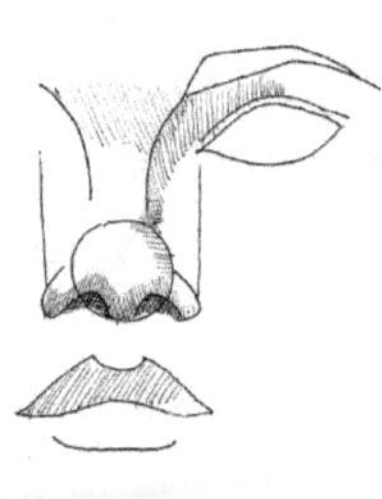

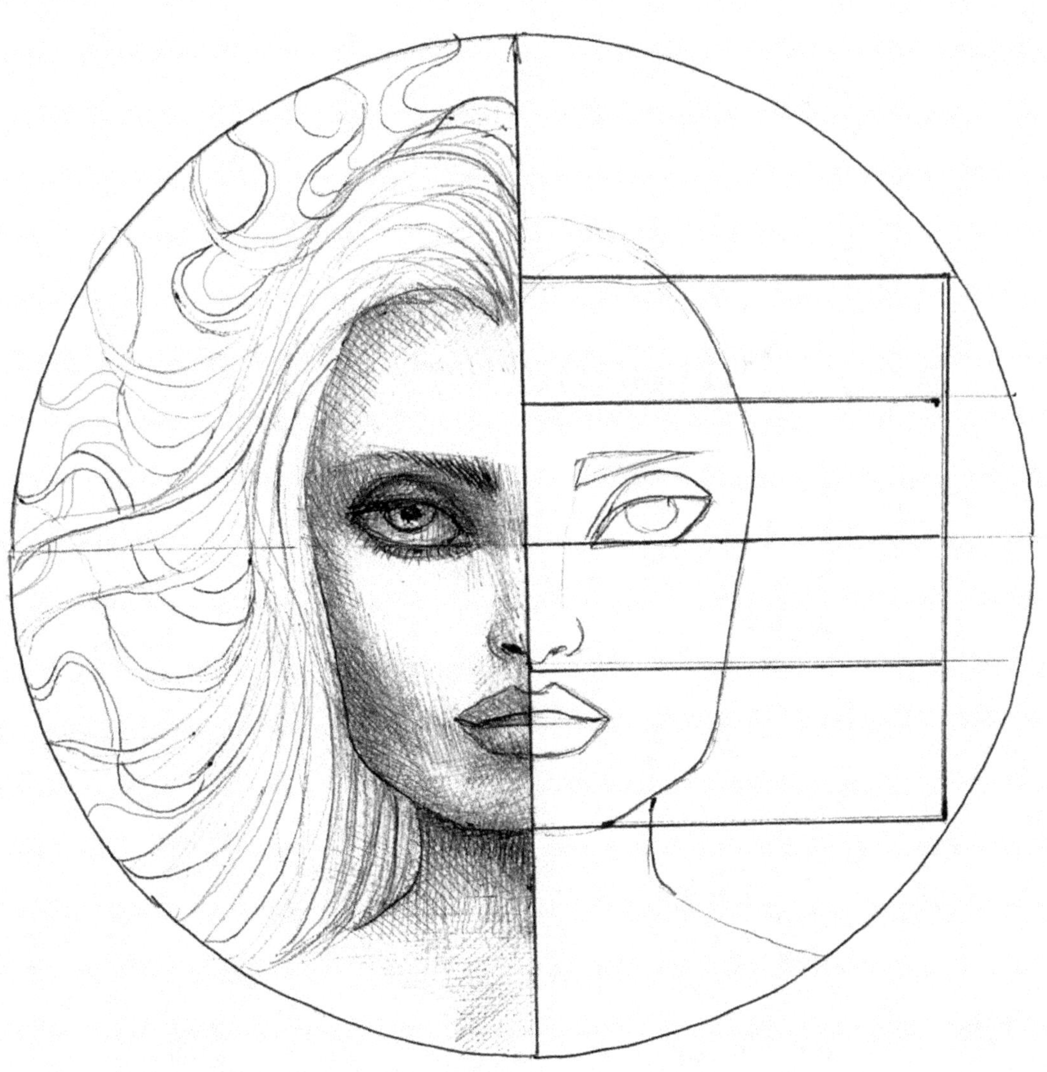

Introduction

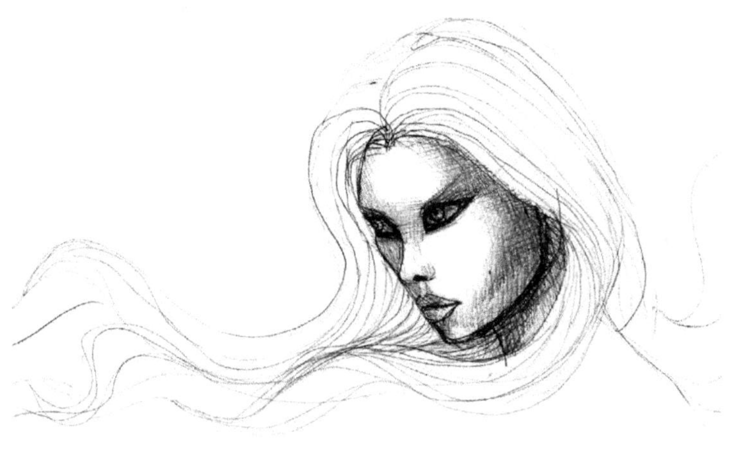

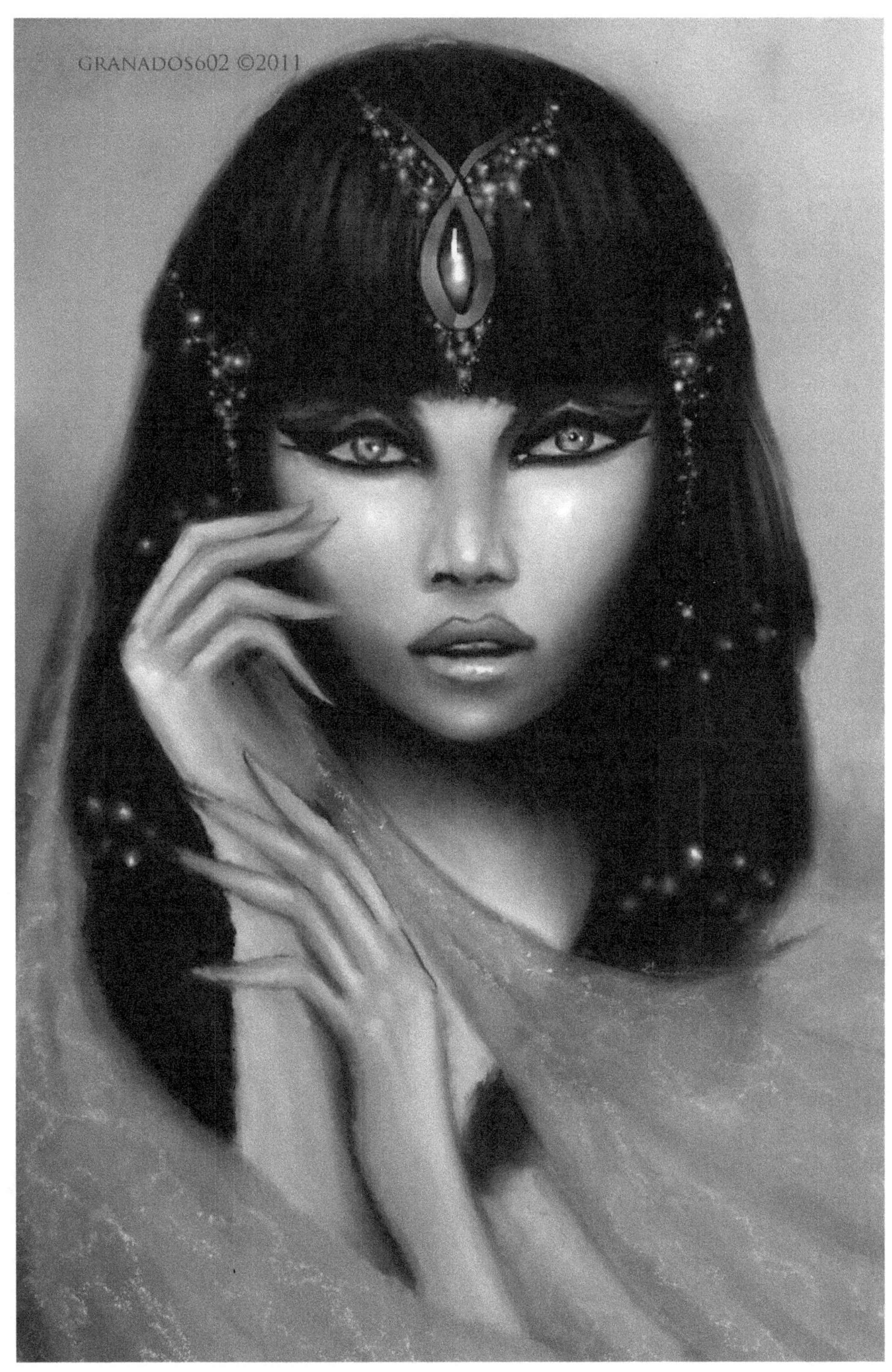
GRANADOS602 ©2011

It has been said, that a face can launch a thousand ships, and that beauty can kill a beast. From the queen of the Nile to the Madonna and child, artist throughout the centuries have depicted enchanting and beguiling female characters. Artists were inspired to paint the female characters from religion, mythology, and legends.

For instance, in religion we have paintings of saints battling demons and dragons. We have souls condemned to a dark and burning atmosphere. There are depictions of beautiful angels soaring in the air. The Virgin Mary was always painted as a beautiful maiden.

In mythology themed art, we find illustrations of dragons and serpents. There are gods that ride winged creatures, and temples that float in the clouds. There is even a beautiful goddess born of the sea.

In legends, we see illustrations of monsters chasing females, like Big Foot and the Lock Ness monster. Many artist painted scenes with legendary women such as Cleopatra and Joan of Arch. They were Strong and beautiful females of the battlefield.

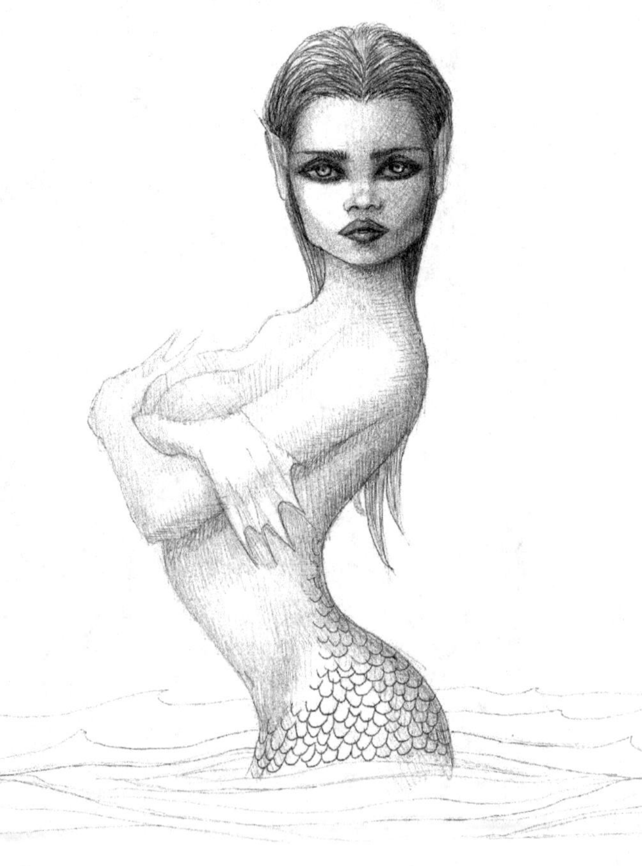

It is easy to understand, why artists in history were inspired by the female characters in these themes. They were able to interpret these themes and characters as creatively as possible. In each of these themes artist have sought to capture the perfect beauty, using the female character as a focal point.

I believe, many of todays fantasy artist also use these female characters as the inspiration source for their own work .

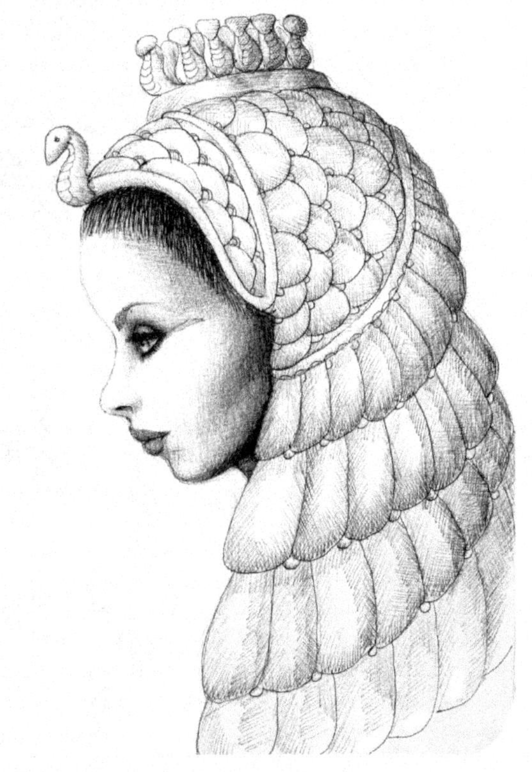

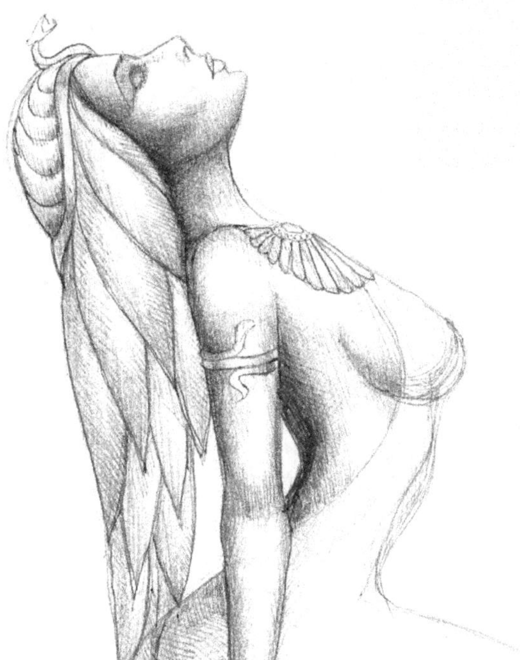

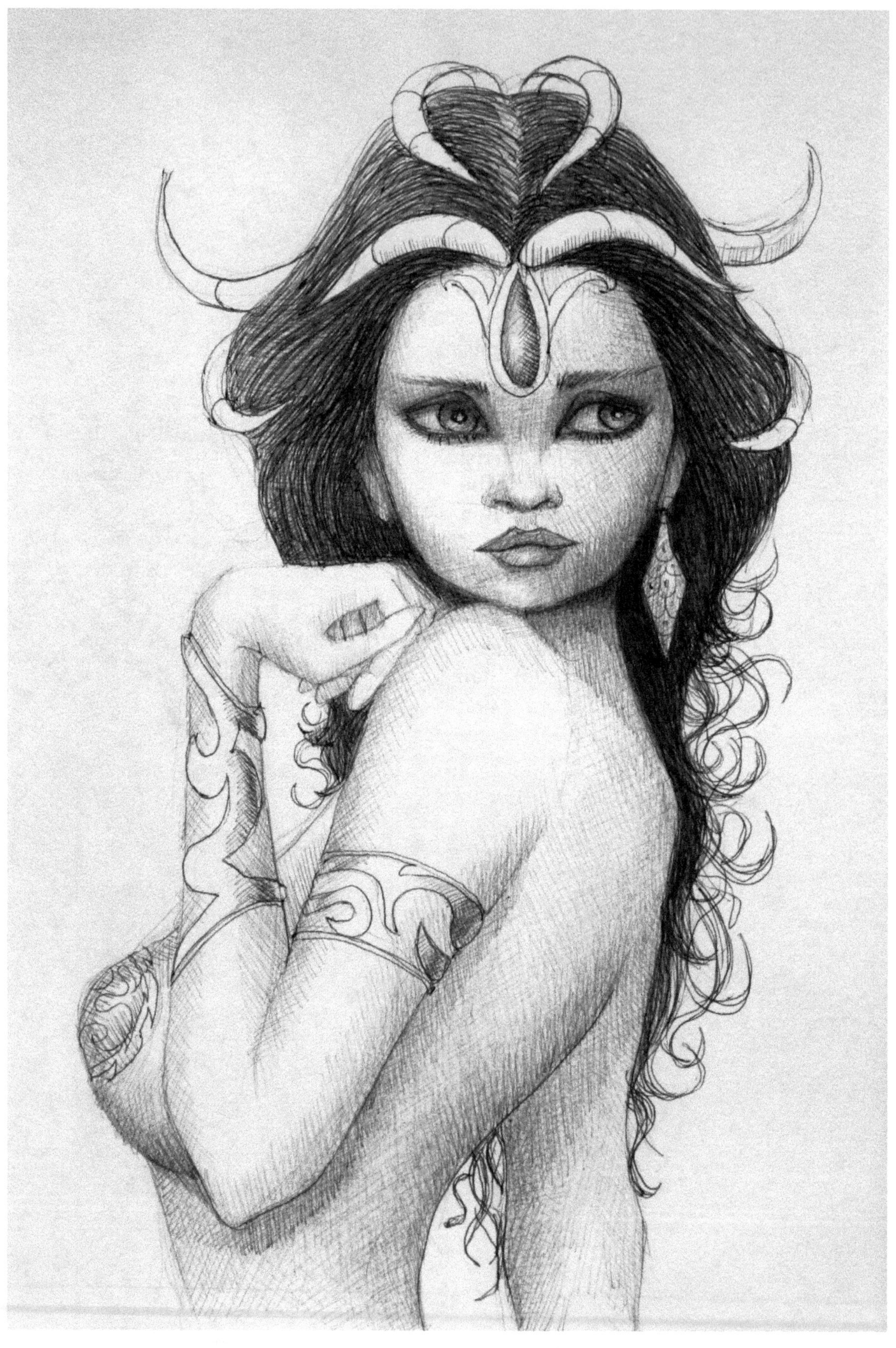

My favorite thing to draw is the female face. When I was a kid in school, I would always draw faces. I would just draw them over and over. In high school, I took a lot of art classes. I learned the basic principals and rules for drawing the human face.

As I got better at drawing many of my friends would have me draw pictures of their family members or their girlfriends. Once a friend of mine had me draw a portrait of his mother for a contest he was going to enter in his name. I reluctantly agreed to do it for him. He took the drawing I did for him, and he entered it in the contest. The drawing won first place, and he got one hundred dollars. I was very excited the drawing I did for him won, but he got all the credit. That is when I stopped drawing portraits of real people, and I decided to mostly concentrate on drawing fantasy faces.

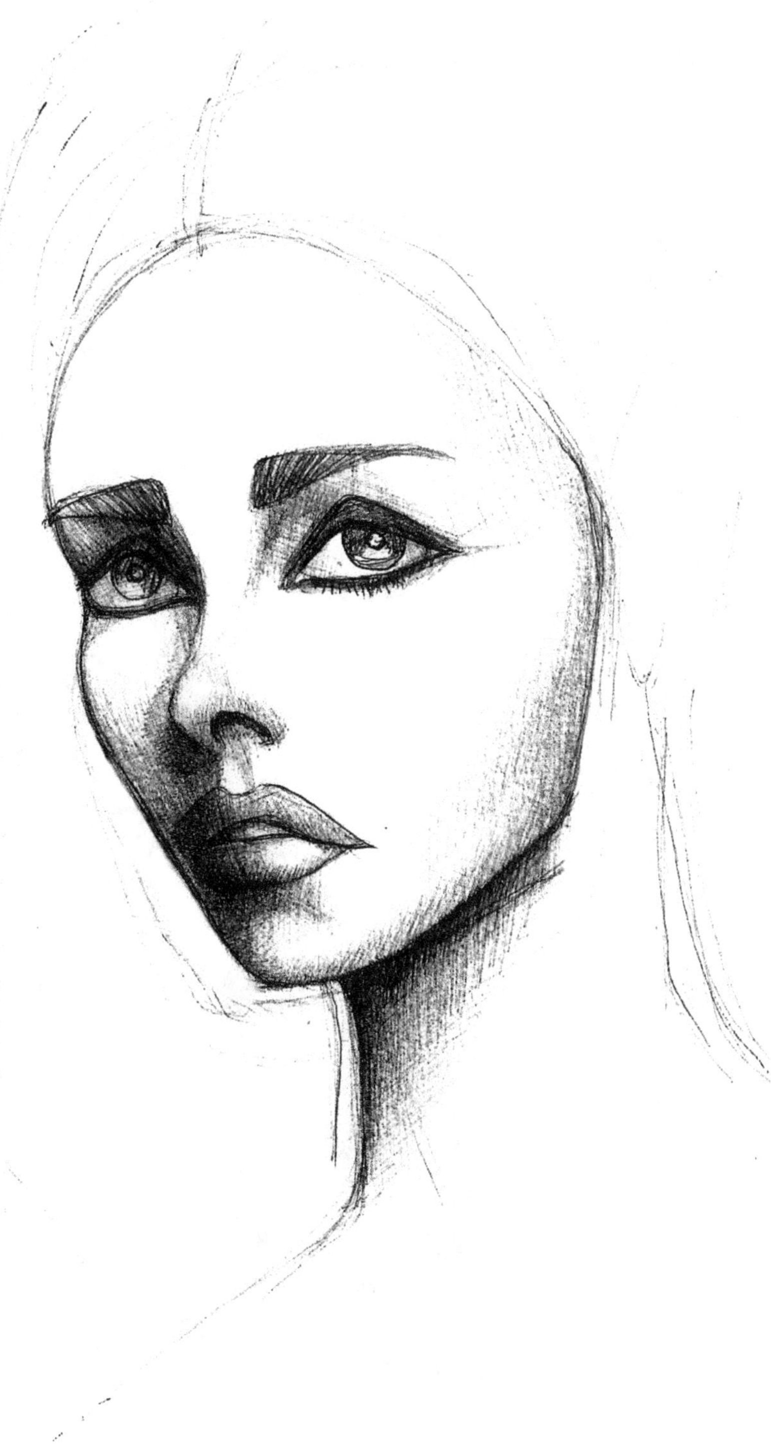

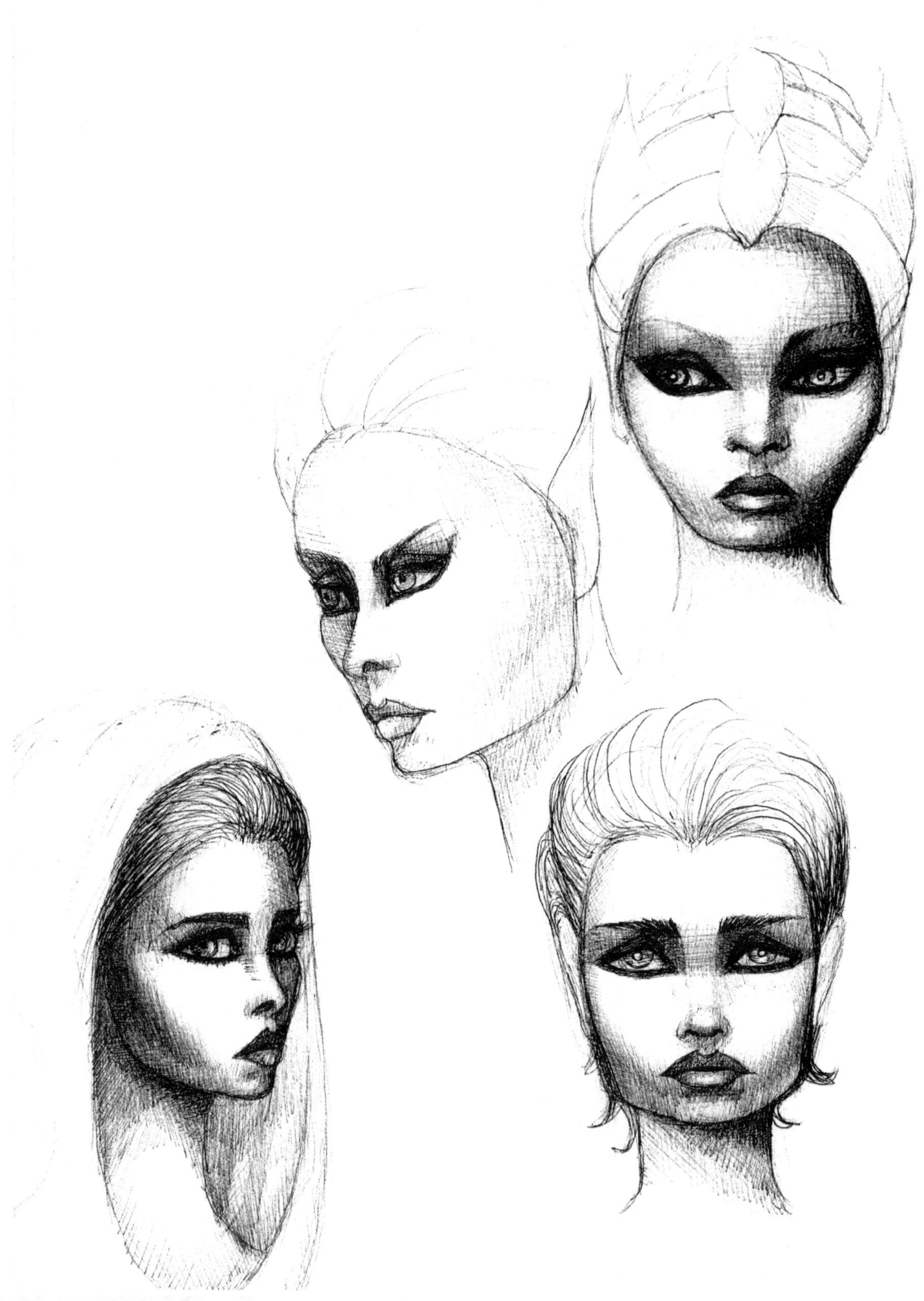

In college, I took art history and fine art classes. It was art history that really fascinated me the most. I was intrigued by how artist used different themes and inspiration in their work.

To me art is not about drawing just what you see. It's about interpreting what you see, and how you see things. I love to look at artwork that shows all the imperfections. I look at how artist interpret their subject. I look at how they draw the lines or how they use color. How they use the lights and darks, and which one is emphasized.

An artist can reflect in his work how one thinks, not just what one thinks. An artist should be able to project a piece of his soul to the viewer. It is like exposing a part of your inner most personal being to the world.

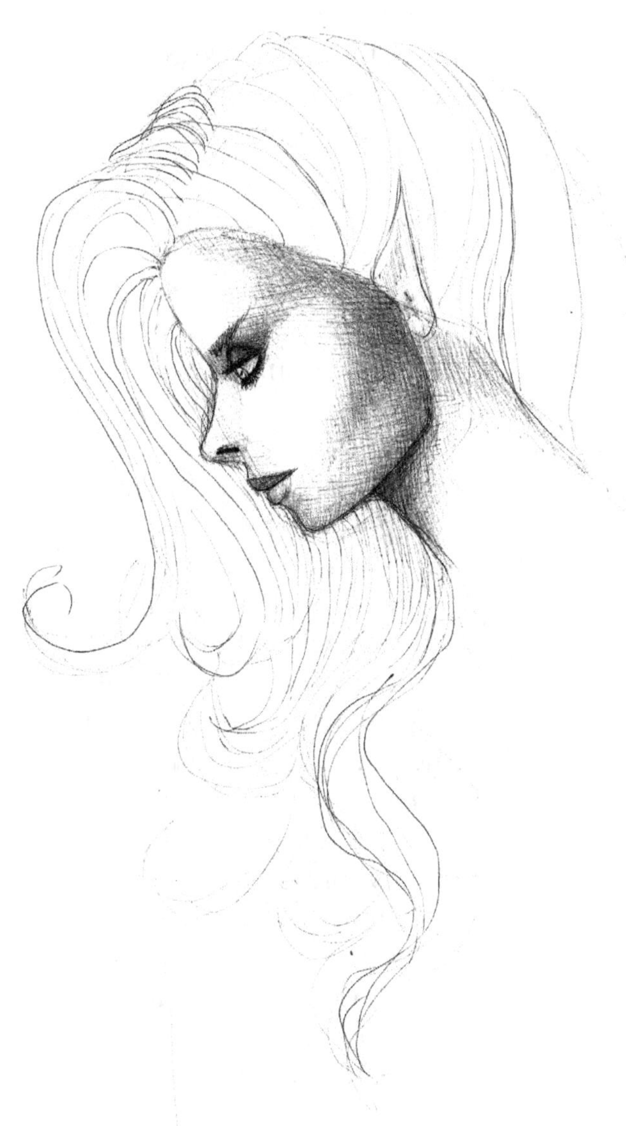

A long time ago, someone once said to me that being an artist is a gift from god. From that moment on, it sort of clicked in for me. I never thought of being an artist in those terms before. So, I made a commitment to dedicate myself, and my life to being an artist. To think of myself as an artist, no matter what I do, or where life takes me. I disciplined myself to painting and practicing my drawing techniques everyday.

Each day I also try to meditate a little. I think of how grateful I am just to be alive, and to be an artist.

I believe, that as a fantasy artist, it helps to be a bit spiritual. You should be able to go deep inside yourself to find your inspiration and imagination. I think every artist should. Otherwise, you are just like a photocopier. Drawing exactly what you see, with no feeling or soul. I see a lot of that from artist who do a lot of straightforward portraiture.

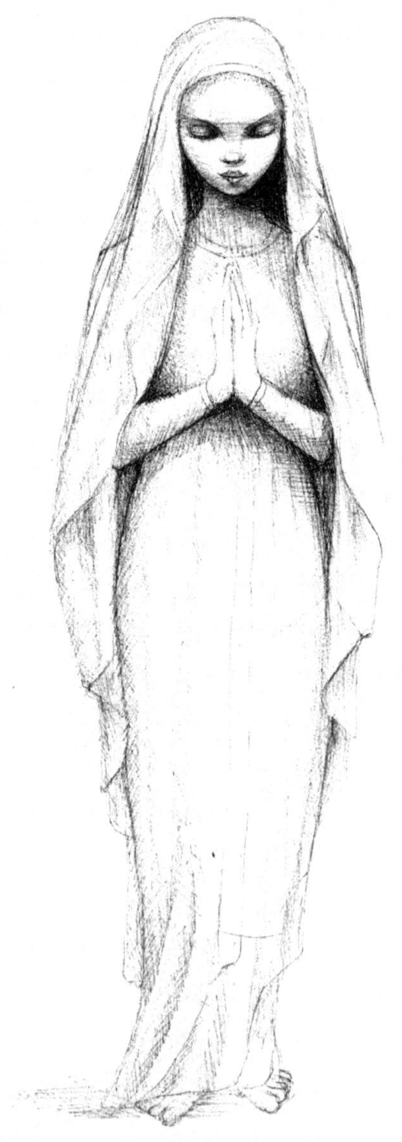

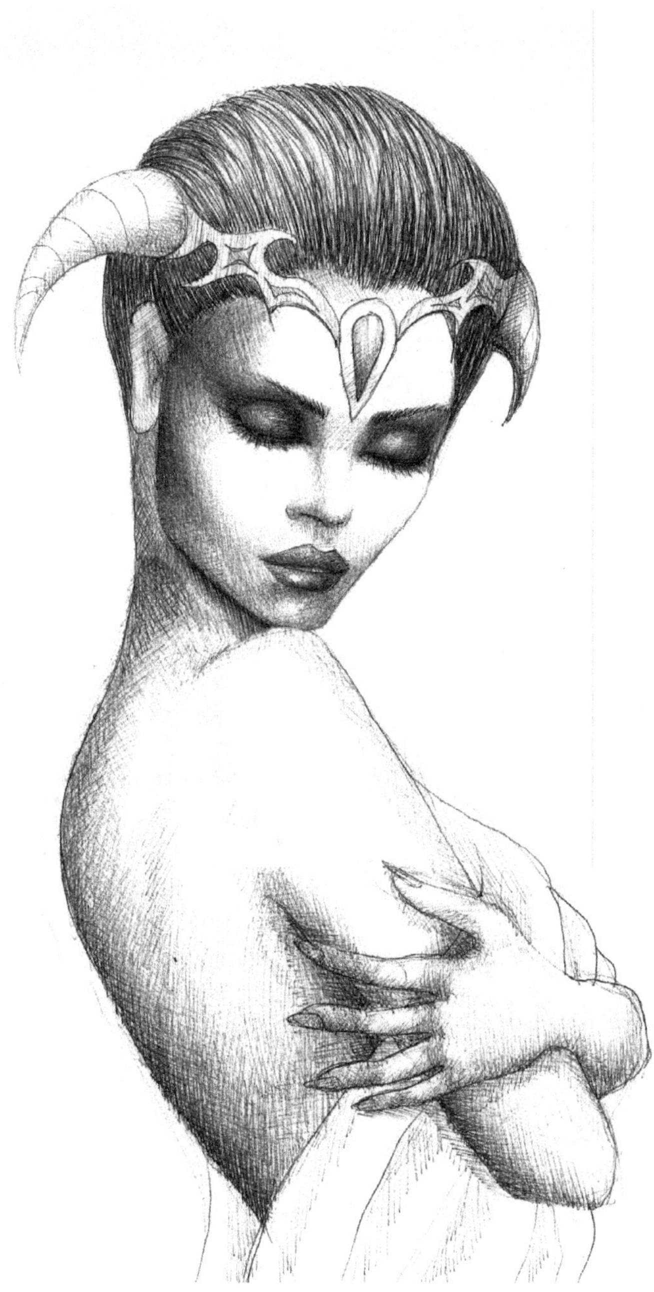

For me, drawing and painting is a form of meditation. I sit still, and then take all of my thoughts and feelings and concentrate them. I focus everything together into a single point. I transfer it to my hand, then to my fingertips. Then I begin to draw, and let all those feeling and thoughts flow on to my sketchpad or canvas.

At that moment, it feels like I have reached a higher level. It is like a place, where I am able to interpret my inner soul. Imagine a world that communicates by using colors, light and darkness, rhythm and motion, sound and silence.

I think of it, as a kind of creative energy source. When you tap into this energy, it will inspire you on a deeper level. Through the use of meditation, you can harness your thoughts and emotions into a highly evolved creative energy source.

Chapter 1
Tools of the trade

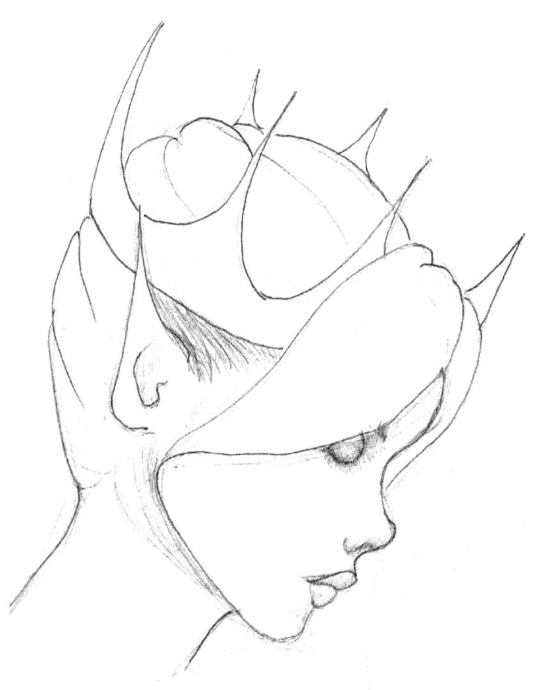

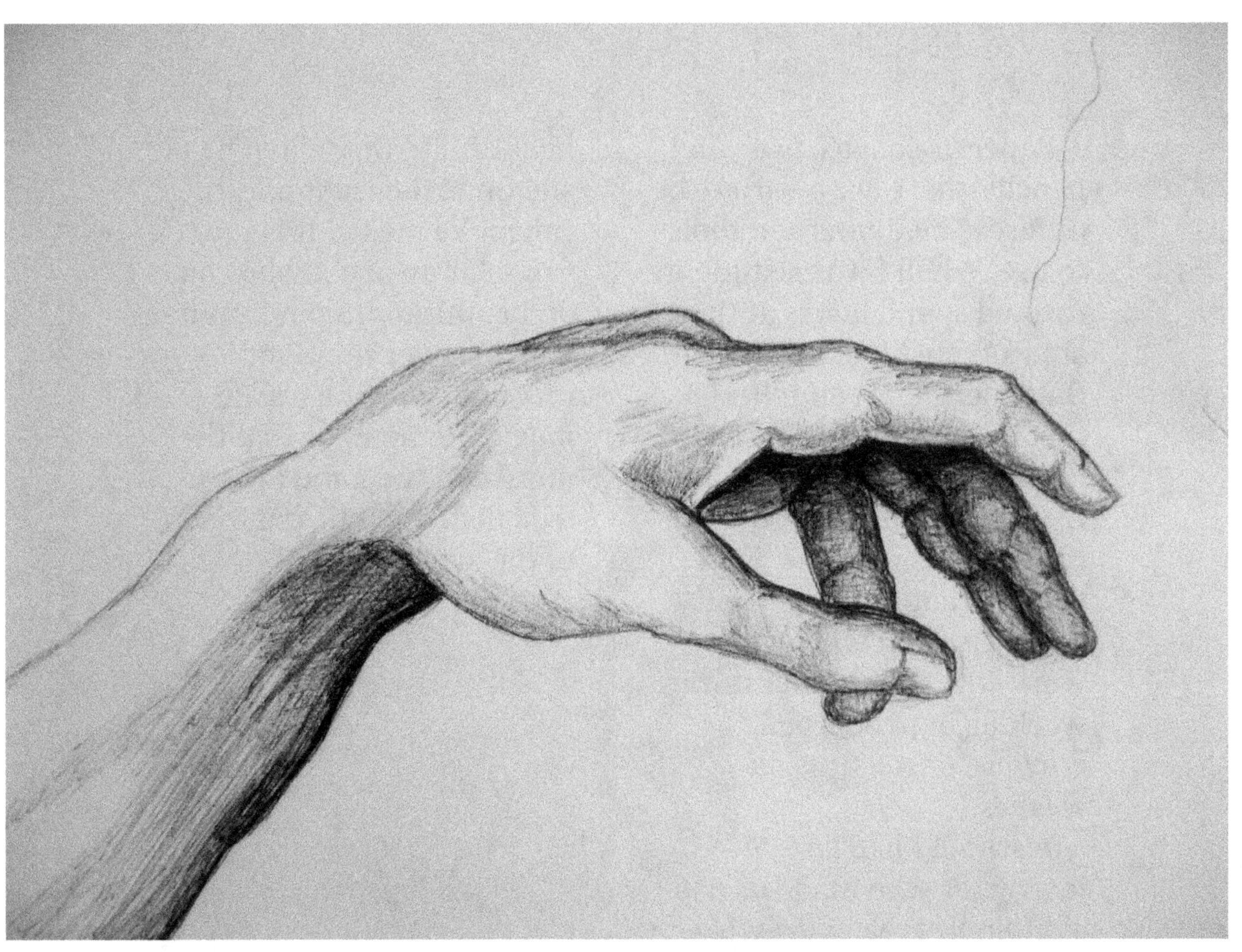

Paper or canvas, pens and pencils, there are a variety of different mediums and tools to use. When I was a student, I would spend hours at the art store just looking at all the different art supplies that were in stock. I think it is a good idea to explore and tryout as many different mediums as possible. Find the one that best suits you, and feels right when you work with it. Whether it is working in pencil, pen, crayons, pastels, or ink washes.

In school I had an instructor who made us use a different type of drawing medium every week. She wanted us to experience how each one felt. She would say, "It's like playing a different instrument." As I sat there listening to her, I couldn't help but feel, that your hand and your mind are the true instruments.

Practice drawing every day and you will keep your hand and mind in tune like a delicate violin. A violinist can play any violin beautifully! But, when he or she finds the right one, they can make magic! It is the same for an artist who can do beautiful drawings. When you discover the right medium, you will create magic! Remember that the mind and the hand are the true instruments and tools of the artist.

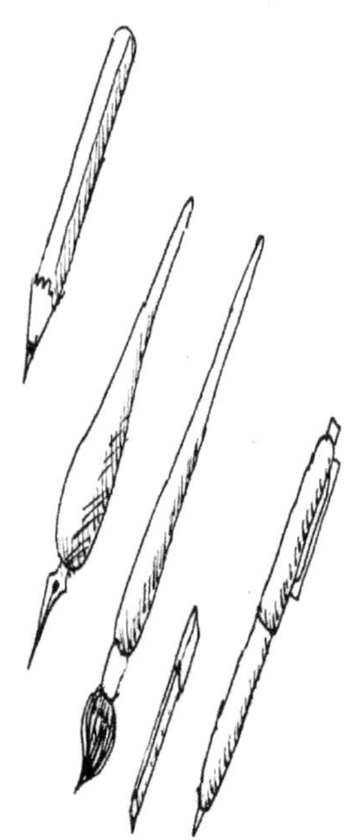

The principal of thinking of your hand and mind as an instrument also applies to the technique that you are using. It is up to you to develop, refine, and master, your artistic skills and talent. Whether your using cross hatching, soft blending, or ink wash techniques, you must practice as much as you can. With practice you will master your technique, only then can your hand and mind be in total control. When you master your technique you will know exactly how to use it, how it behaves as far as its characteristics. You can make it do what you want it to do, and that is the magic of being an artist.

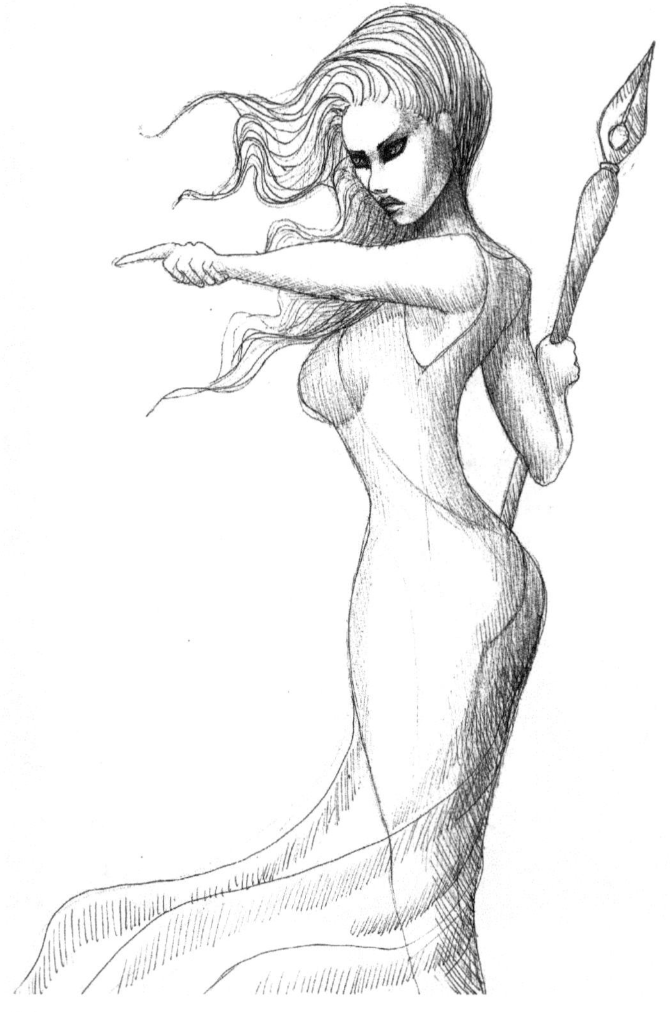

Here are just a few examples of techniques:

Cross Hatching: Crisp clean lines.

Soft Blending: Smooth shading

Coarse Blending: Dark strong blending

Ink Wash: Deep and soft shading

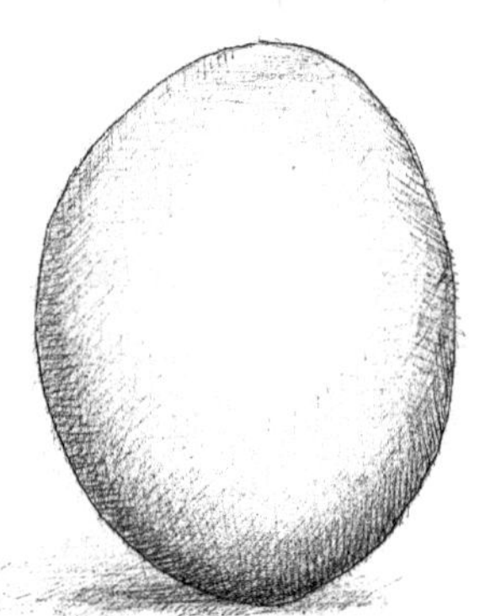

CROSS HATCH TECHNIQUE

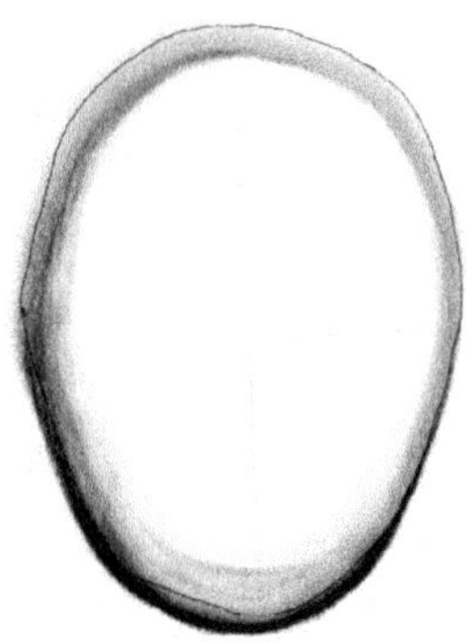

INK WASH TECHNIQUE

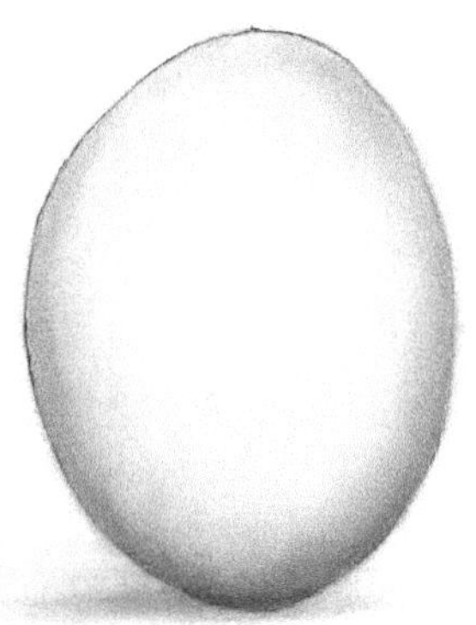

SOFT BLENDING TECHNIQUE

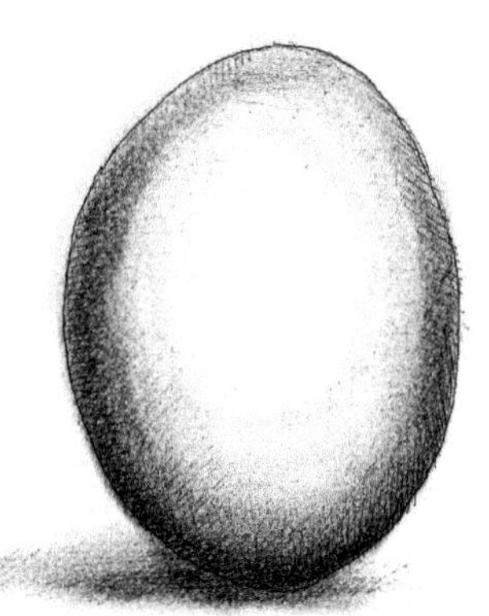

CHARCOAL TECHNIQUE

- It is a good idea to practice drawing and shading basic shapes , such as circles , squares , triangles , ovals and tubular objects .

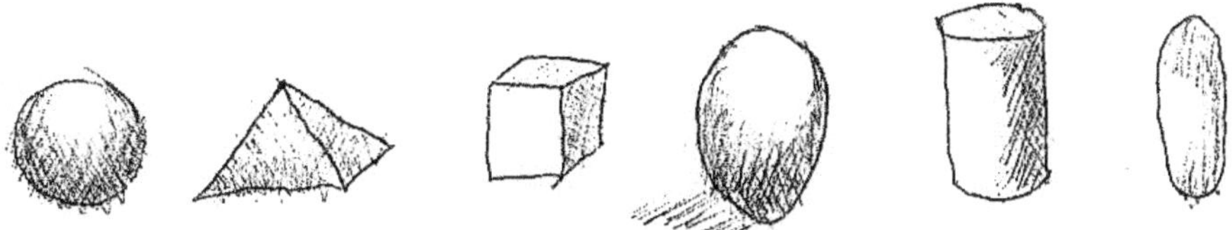

- These are just a few of the basic shapes that make up everyday objects .

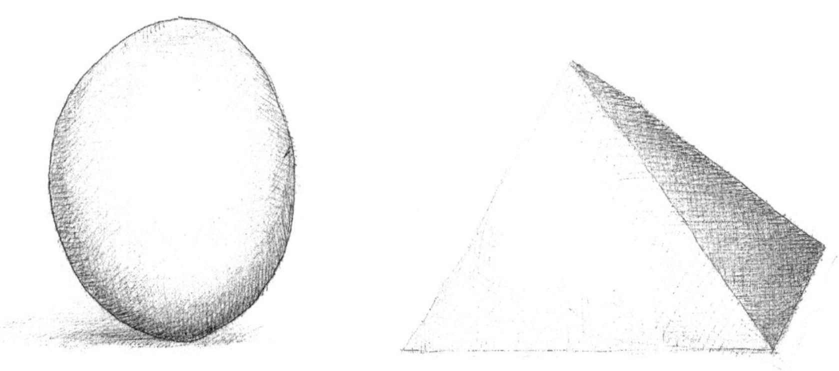

- Practice your shading technique using a bar scale drawing , going from dark to light

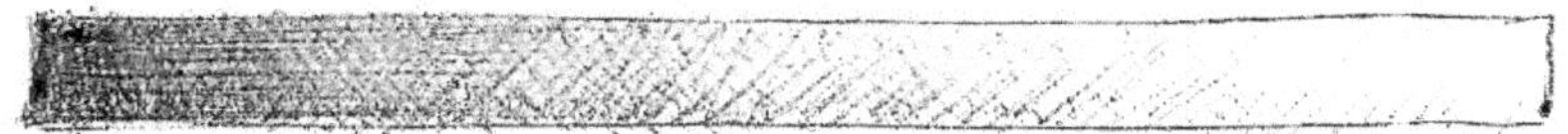

Chapter 2
The Female Fantasy Face

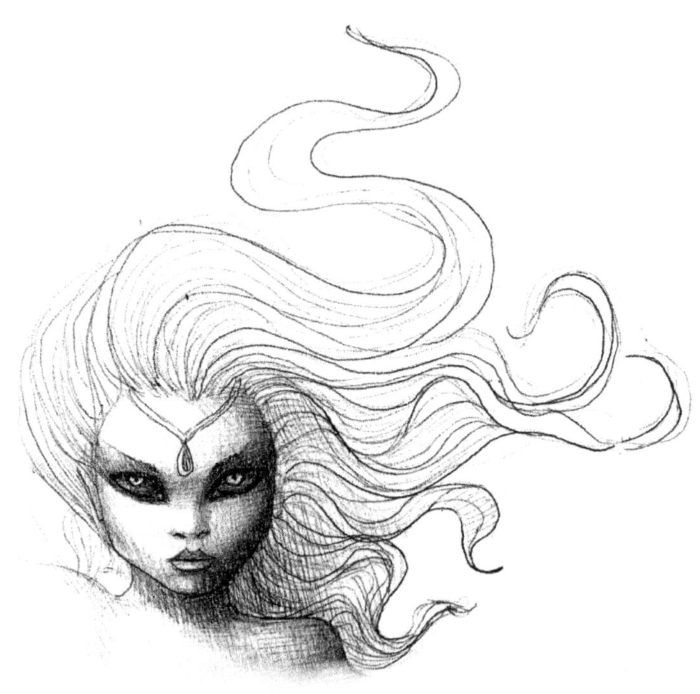

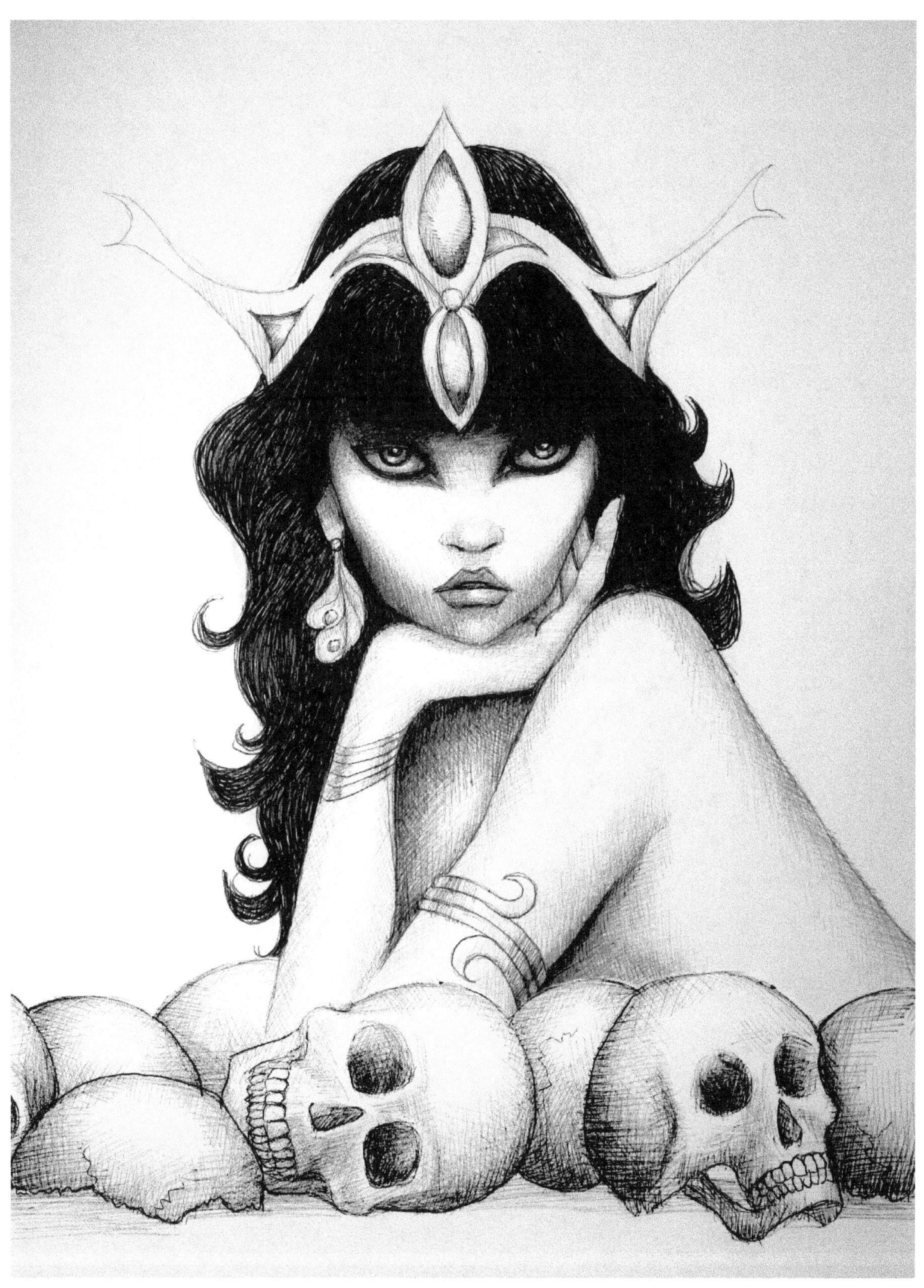

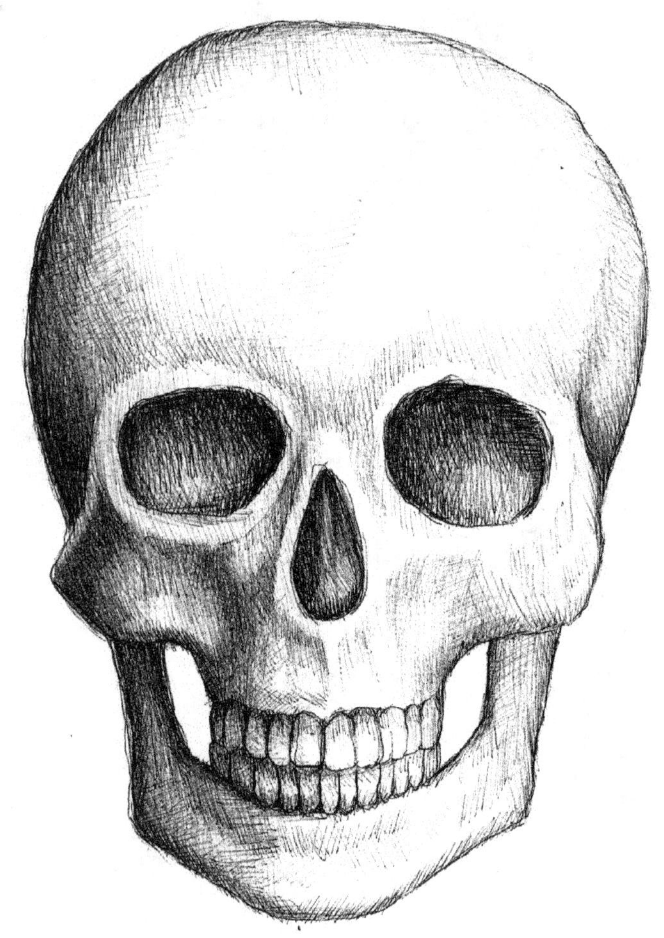

Although, this book is not about the anatomy of the head. I recommend that you practice drawing the skull a few times.

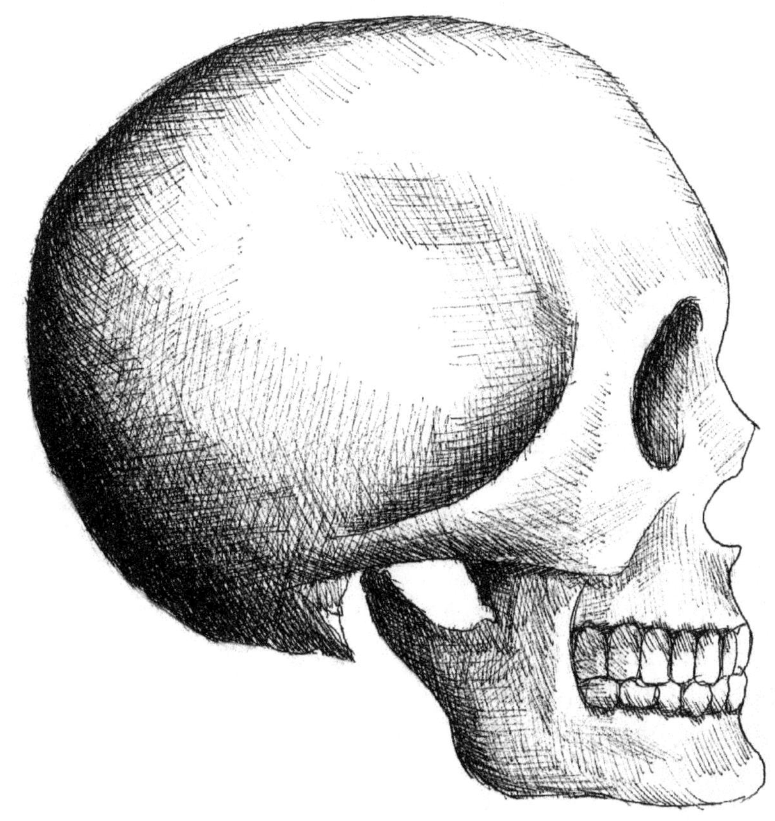

A basic understanding of the skull will help in drawing the face.

In it's most basic form, the female face is just a simple oval with several variations that range from a block to a circle. Therefore, it is a good idea to master drawing ovals and their variations. One of the best methods for this is to simply practice drawing an egg. The egg is one of the best examples of an oval. Just look at it, and study how the light falls on it. Study how the shadows react to its delicate curvatures. Examine how it reflects the light in different lighting scenarios. Carry a small sketchpad with you, and just practice drawing its unique and beautiful shape. The egg, with its delicate and simple beauty, can teach us so much about the art of drawing faces.

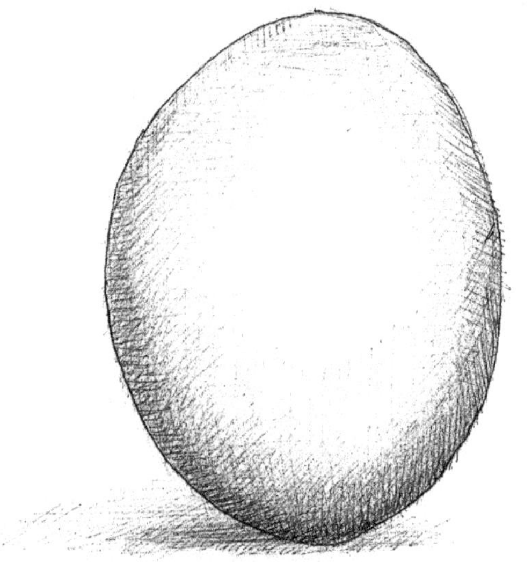

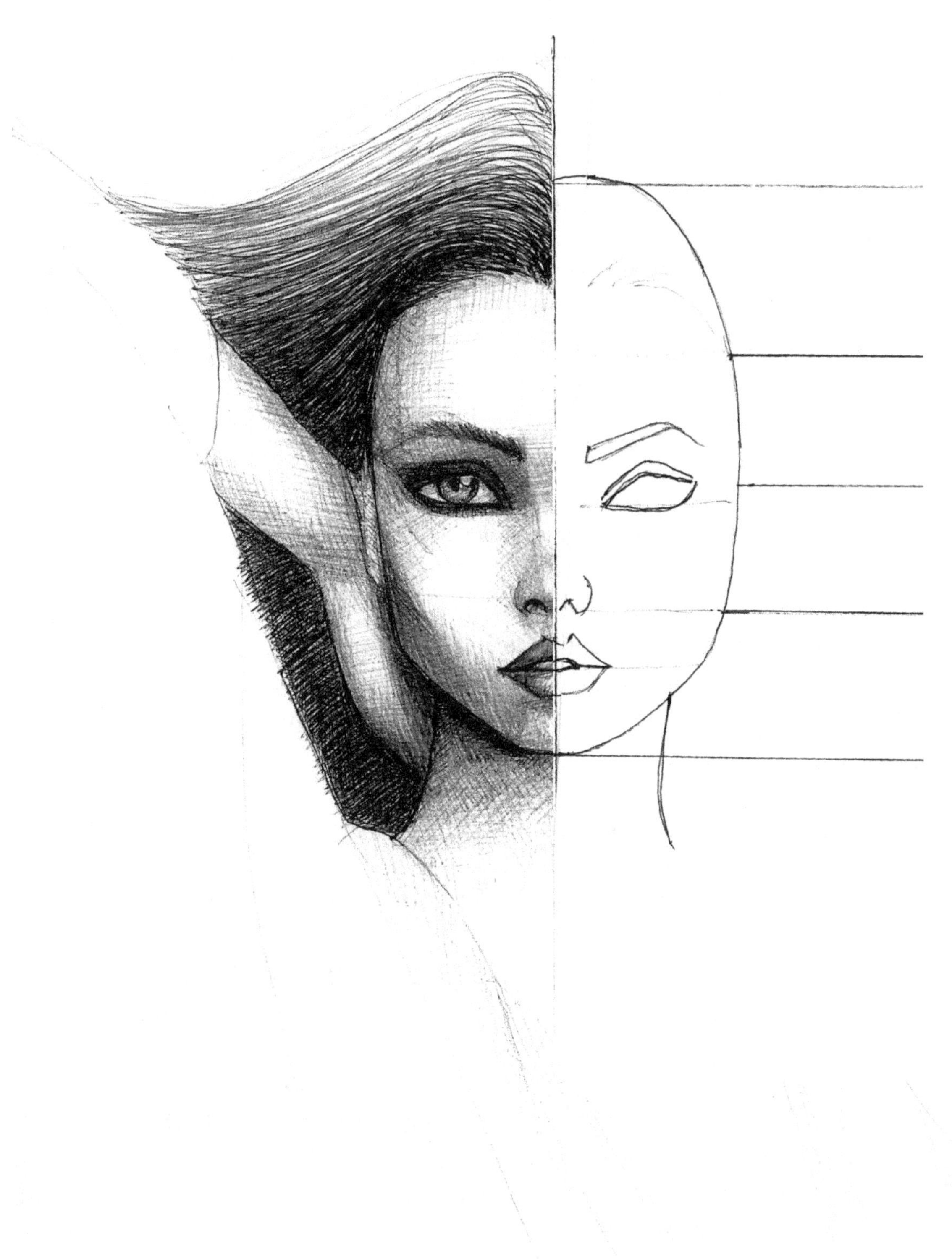

Here is an outline of the steps I use as my guide in drawing the female fantasy face.

- Step one

Begin the face by drawing an oval.

- Step two

Divide it into halves.

- Step three

Divide each half again

- Step four

Draw a small rectangle to indicate the nose
In the center of the lower center half of the oval.

- Step five

Divide in half from the bottom of the rectangle to the bottom of the oval.

This will serve as a basic outline for drawing the female face. Each division will indicate a placement of a facial feature. Now you are ready to draw in the eyes, nose, mouth, and the hairline.

- I like to draw in the eyes first. Place them in the centerline of the oval exactly on each side of the rectangle. Use the centerline as your guide. I usually draw the eyebrows last
- At the bottom of the rectangle I draw in the tip of the nose and the nostrils. I prefer to keep the nose as simple as possible but you can draw the whole thing if you like.
- Place the lips on top of the center division between the bottom of the rectangle and bottom of the oval. Note that you my have to adjust the placement higher or lower, this is a delicate area when drawing female faces. Center the lips between the pupils of the eyes
- Place the hairline on the top most division of the oval.

Figure: 1

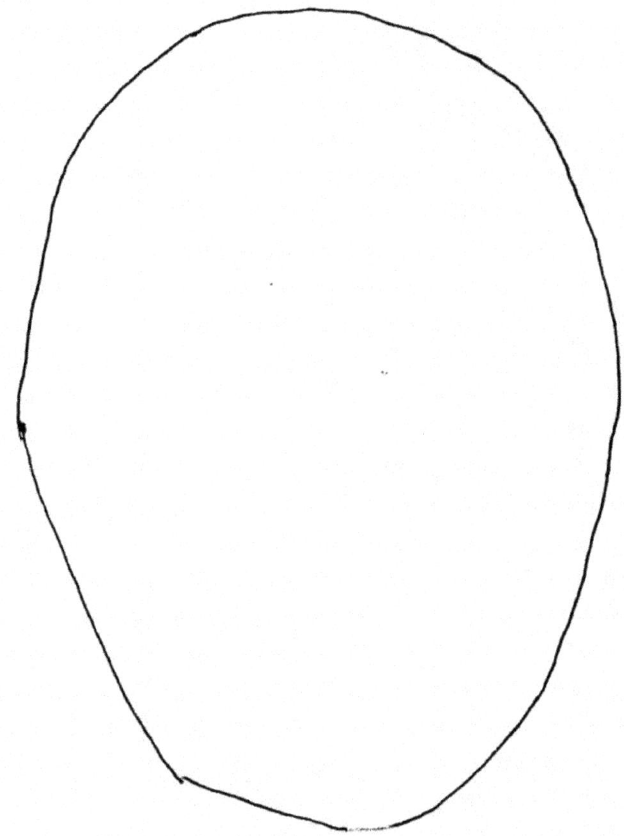

Begin the face by drawing an oval. Your oval does not have to be perfect. Human faces are not either.

Figure: 2

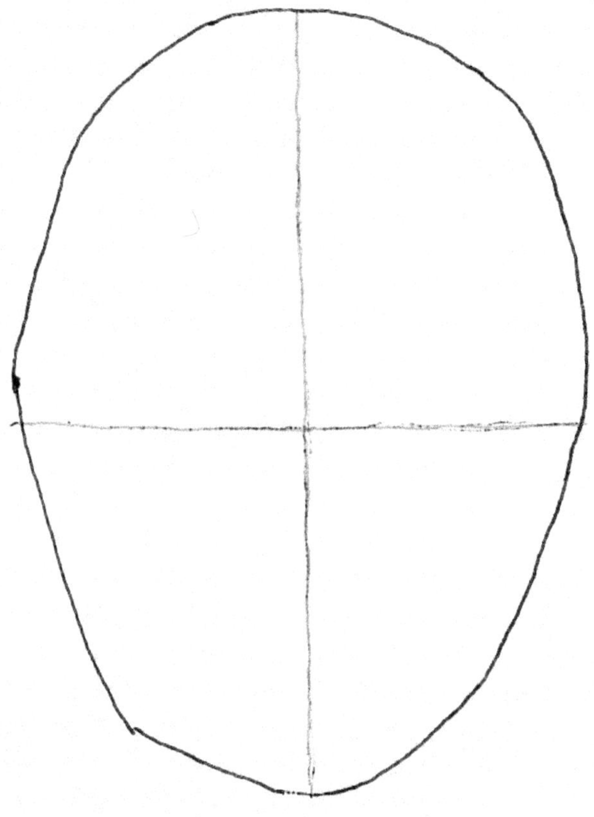

Divide the face vertically in half.
Then divide it horizontally in half.

Figure: 3

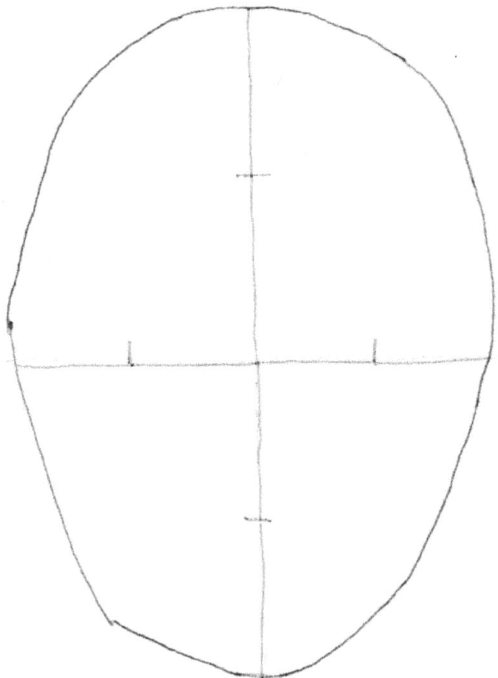

Now, mark each intersecting line approximately in half.

Figure: 4

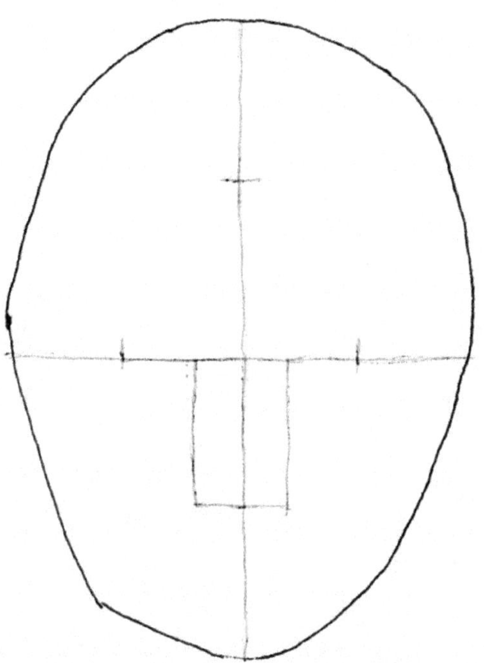

Draw a small rectangle in the center lower half. This will be your guide for the nose and separation guide for the eyes.

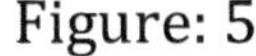

Figure: 5

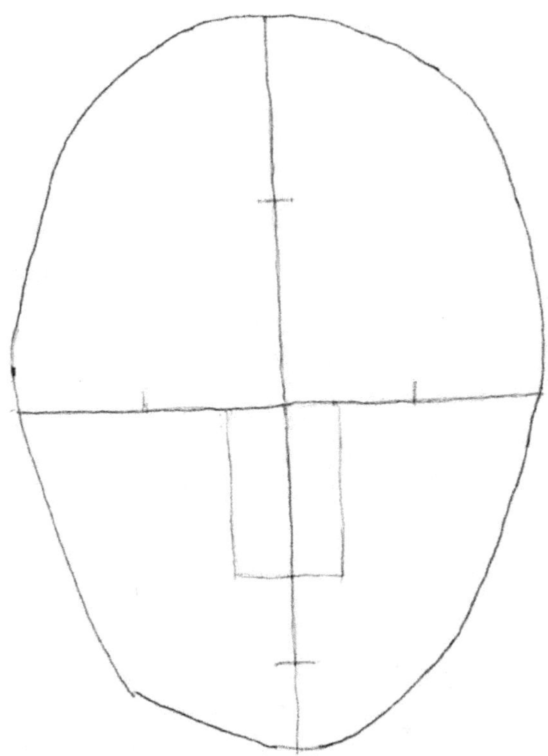

Divide approximately half way from the bottom of the rectangle to the bottom of the oval. Draw a small division line to serve as the lip placement guide.

Figure: 6

Now, you can start to place all the facial features in.

Place the eyes on the center horizontal division line on each side of the nose rectangle.

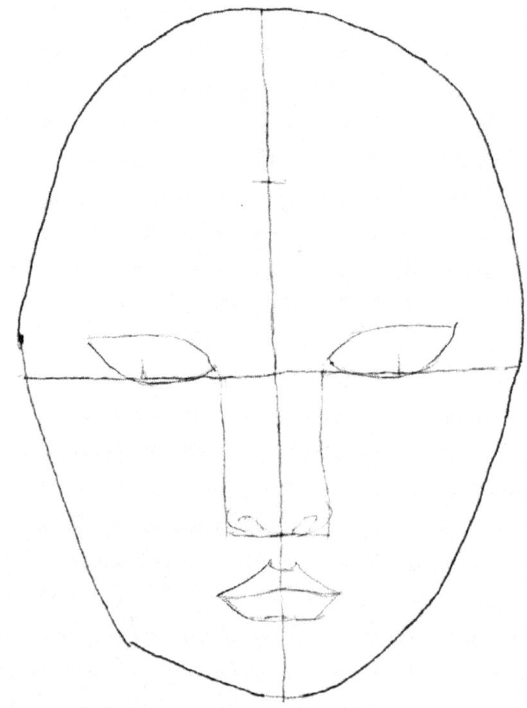

Just draw the tip of the nose in the nose rectangle

Place the lips on the lip line. Use the vertical line to center them in place. You can draw the lips wide or narrow, big or small.

Figure: 7-8

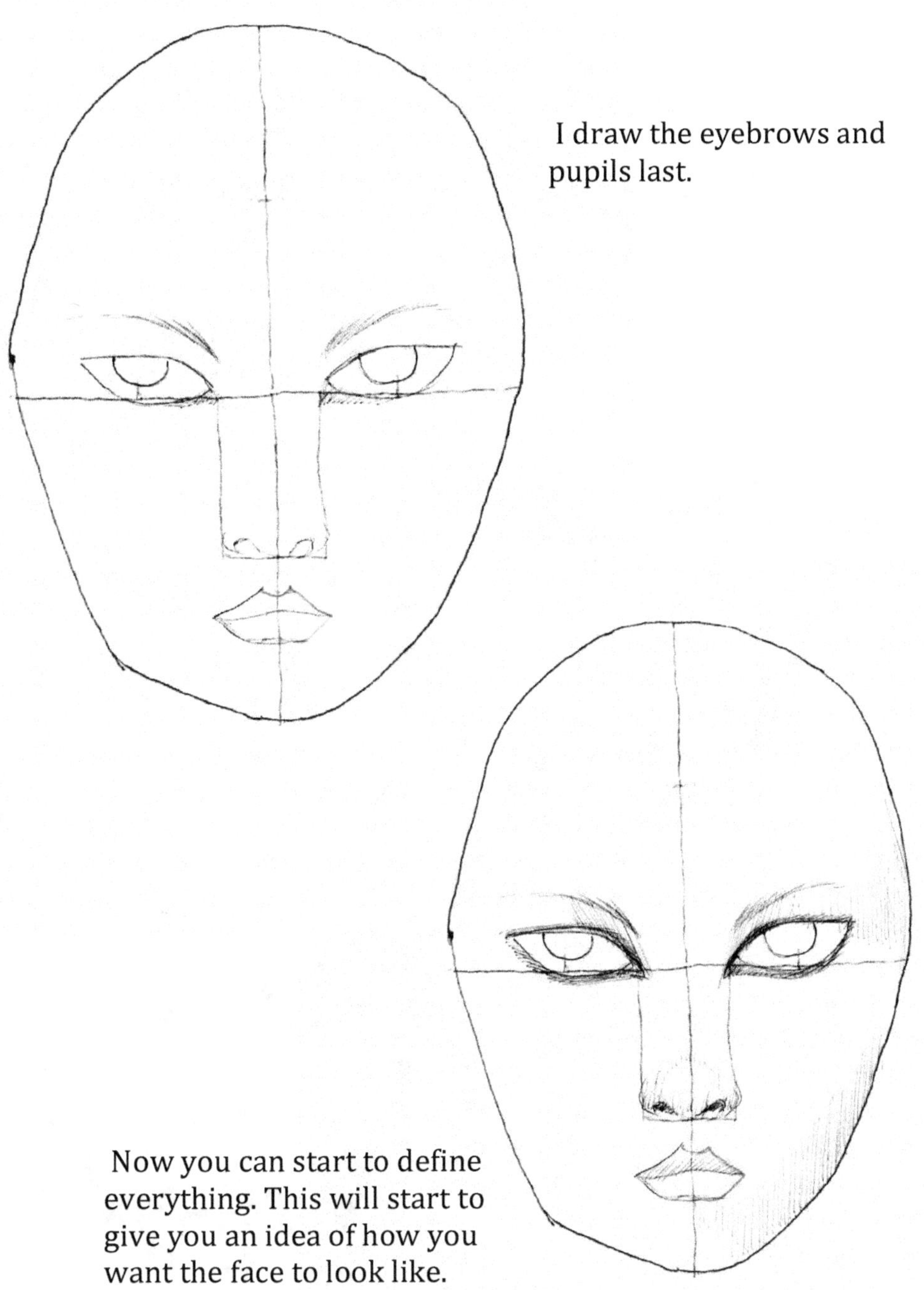

I draw the eyebrows and pupils last.

Now you can start to define everything. This will start to give you an idea of how you want the face to look like.

Figure: 9-10

Determine where your light source is coming from. Start to shade the face accordingly.

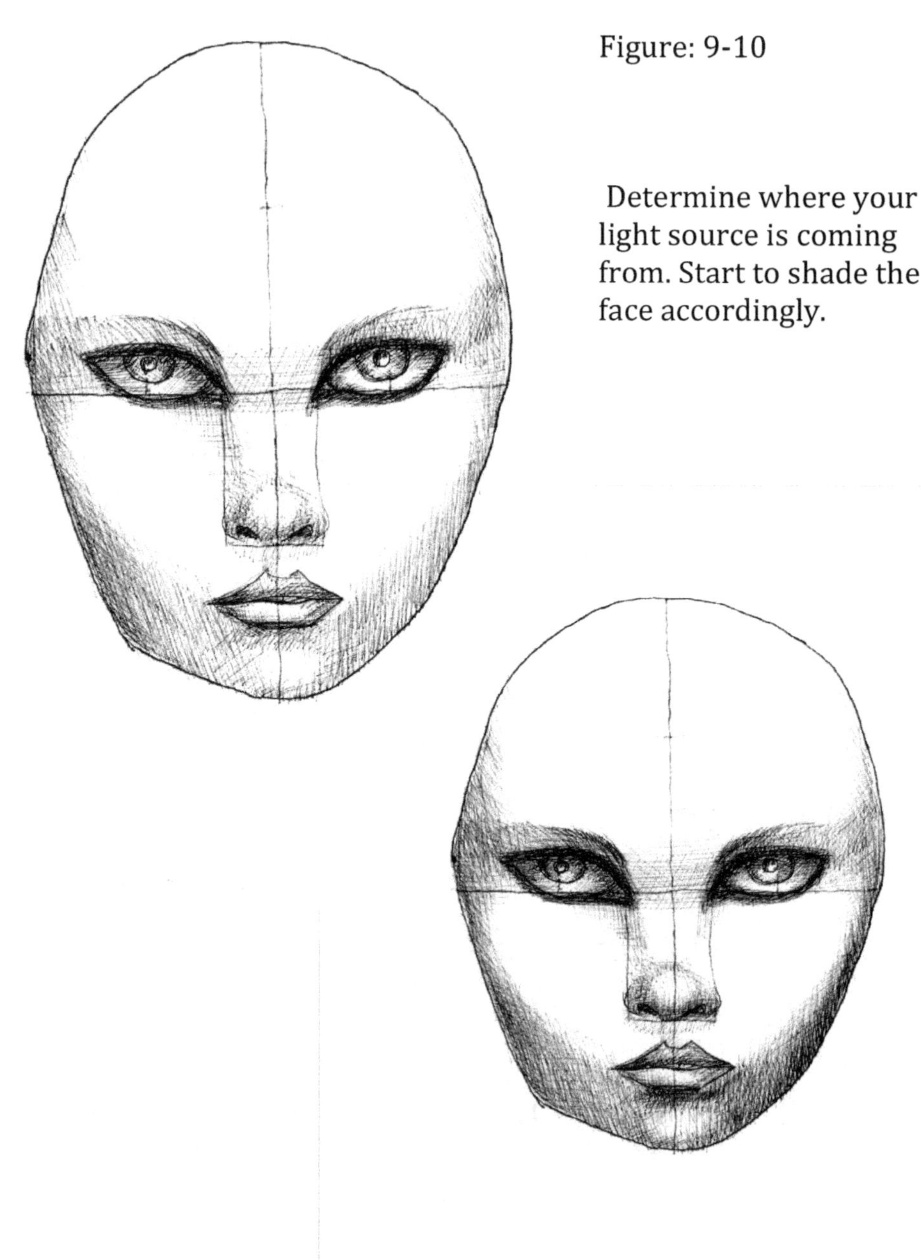

Figure: 11-12

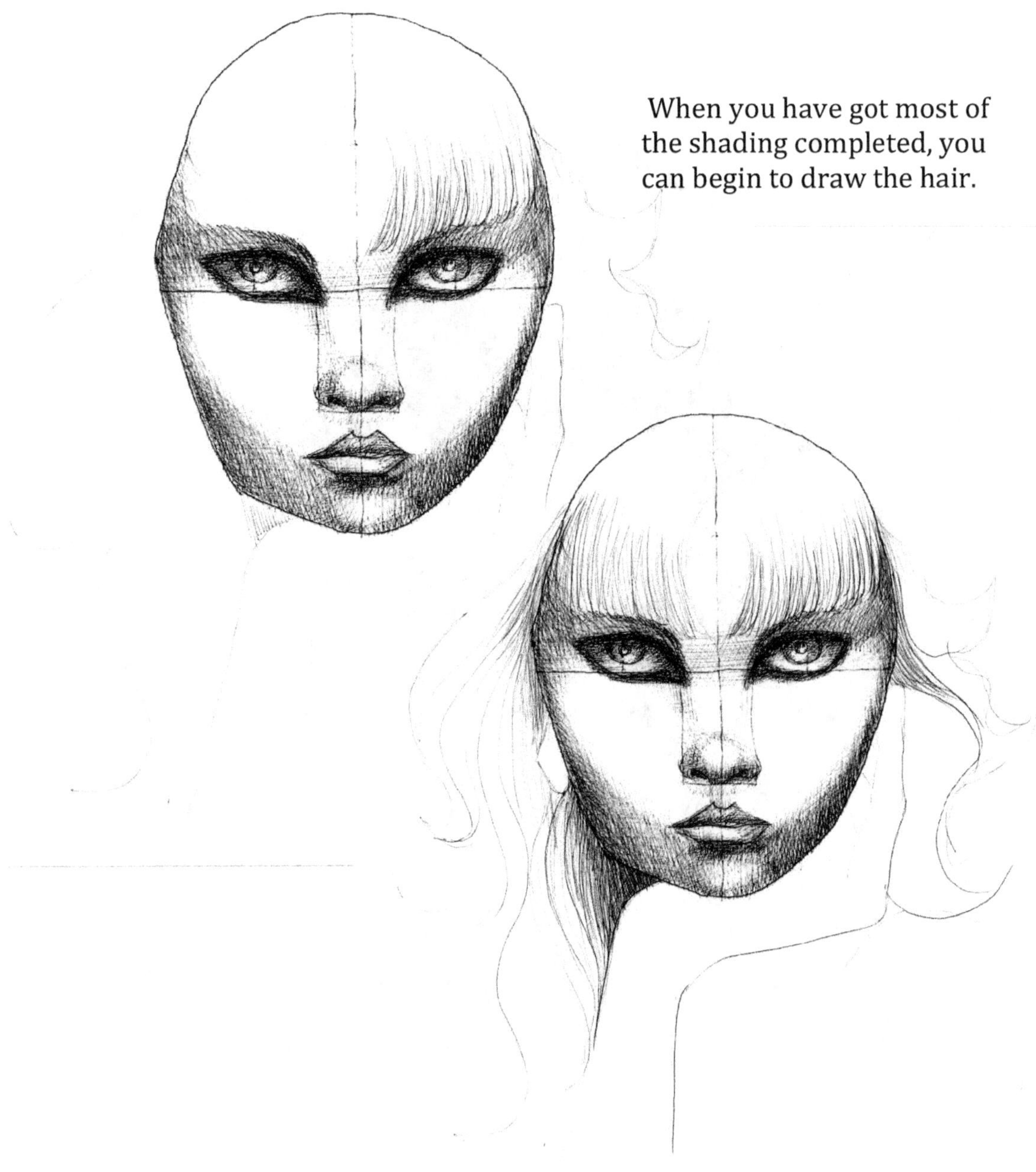

When you have got most of the shading completed, you can begin to draw the hair.

Figure: 13

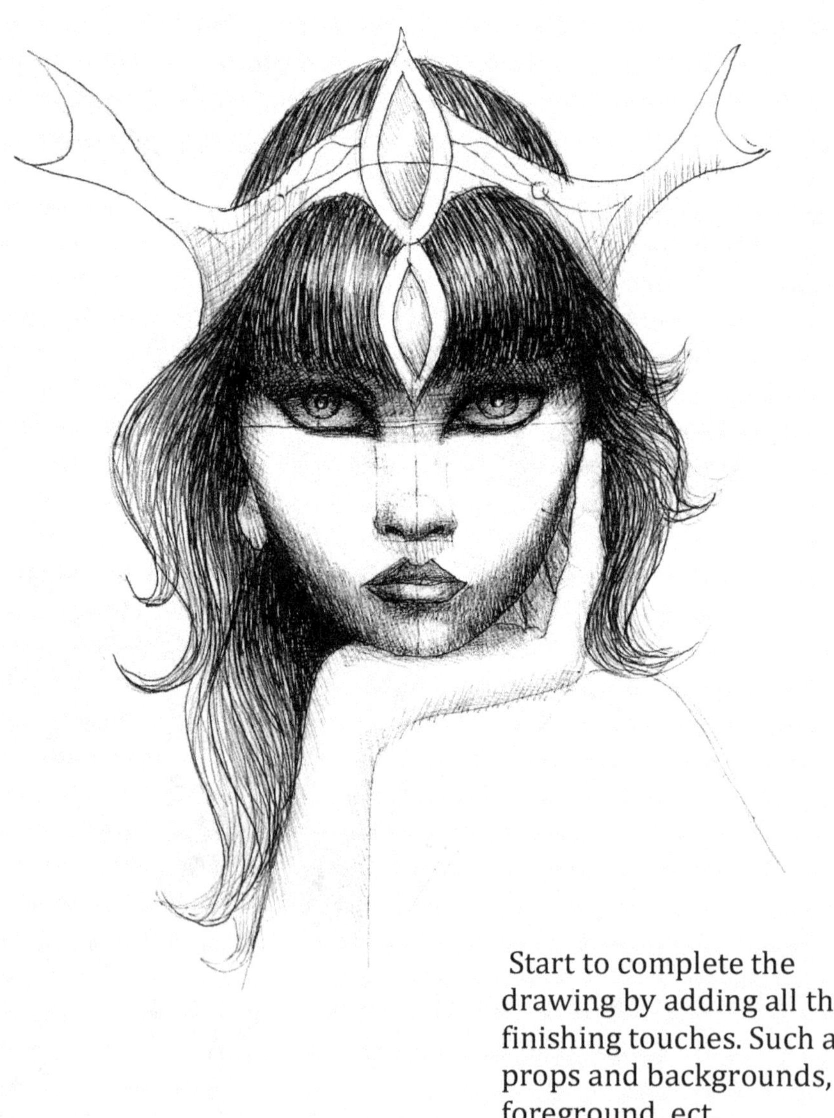

Start to complete the drawing by adding all the finishing touches. Such as props and backgrounds, foreground, ect.

Gaining drawing experience is very important when learning to draw female faces. I recommend that you memorize the guidelines and steps I have outlined . Practice drawing the female face using these guides as much as you can. Don't worry about drawing everything perfectly. The key is to keep drawing as much as you can and if you make mistakes don't erase them. Study and learn from your mistakes and try to incorporate them into the drawing. In time you will be able to correct your mistakes by using and developing your shading techniques. Remember that every time you start over with a new drawing you gain valuable experience .

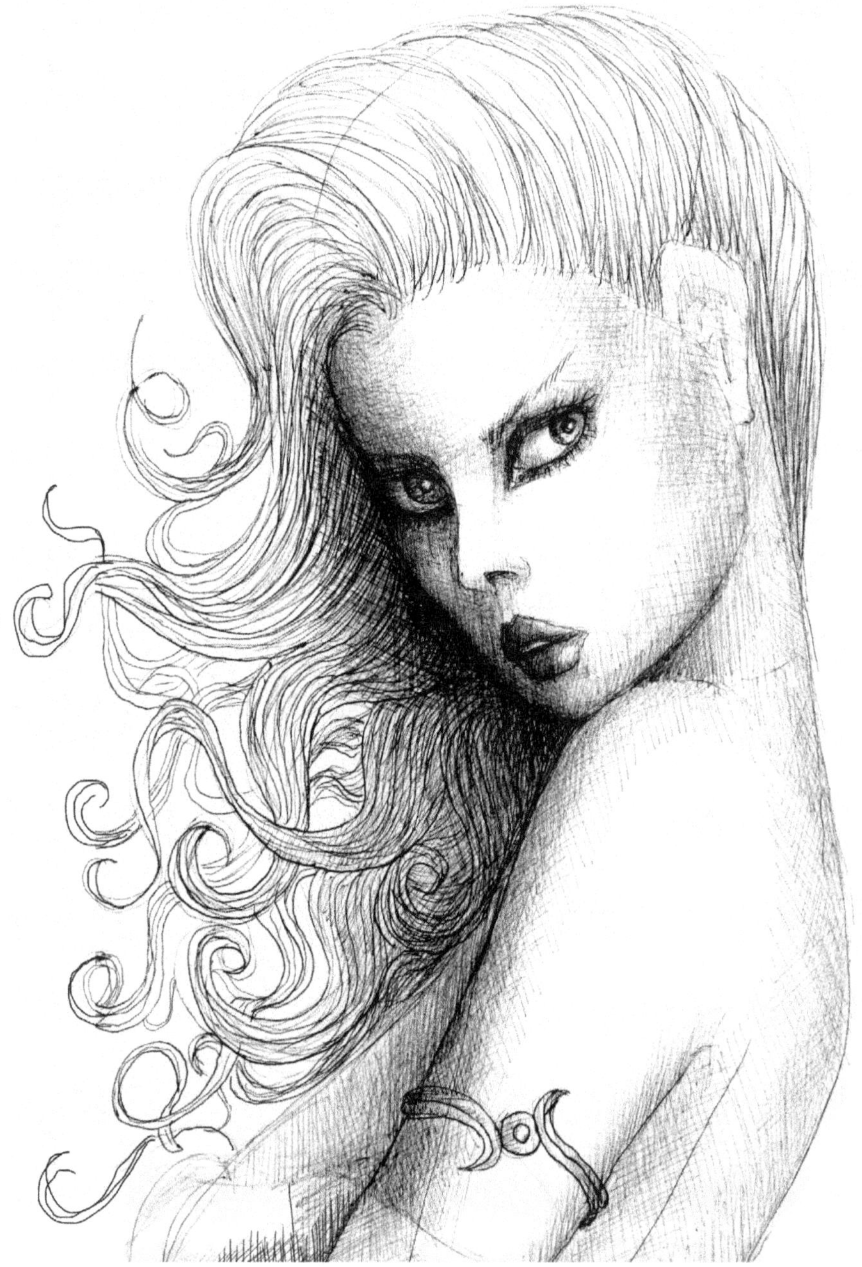

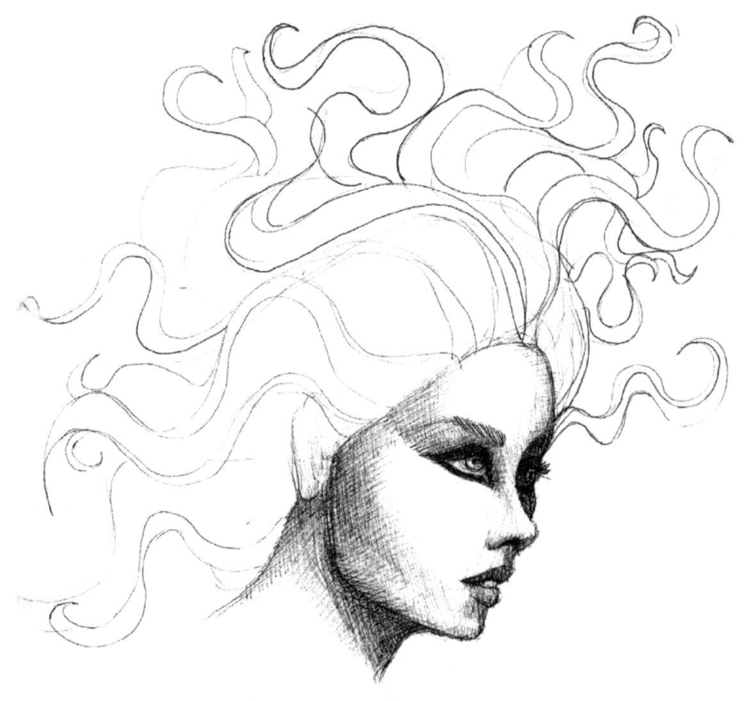

Chapter 3
Profiles Of The Female Fantasy Face

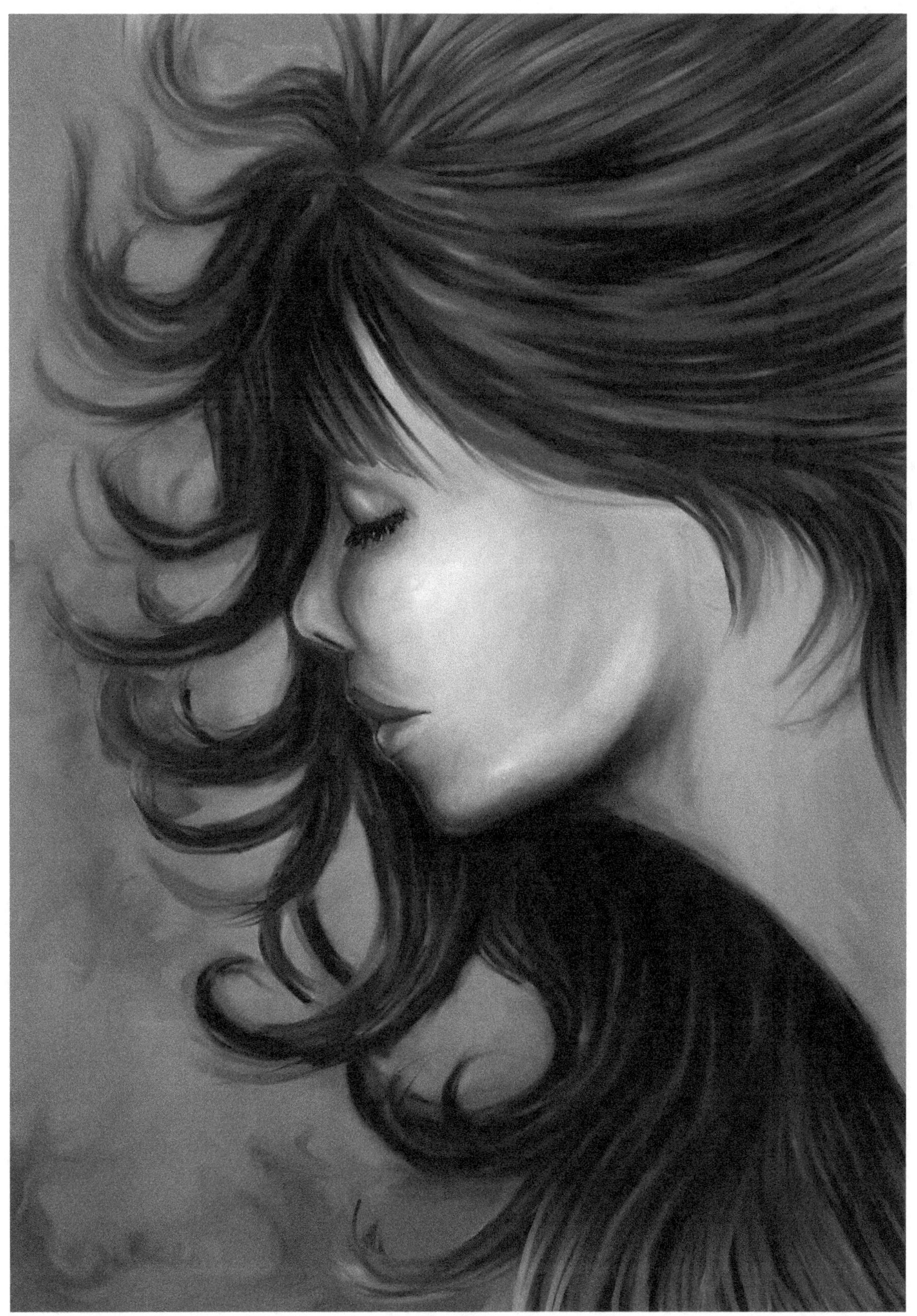

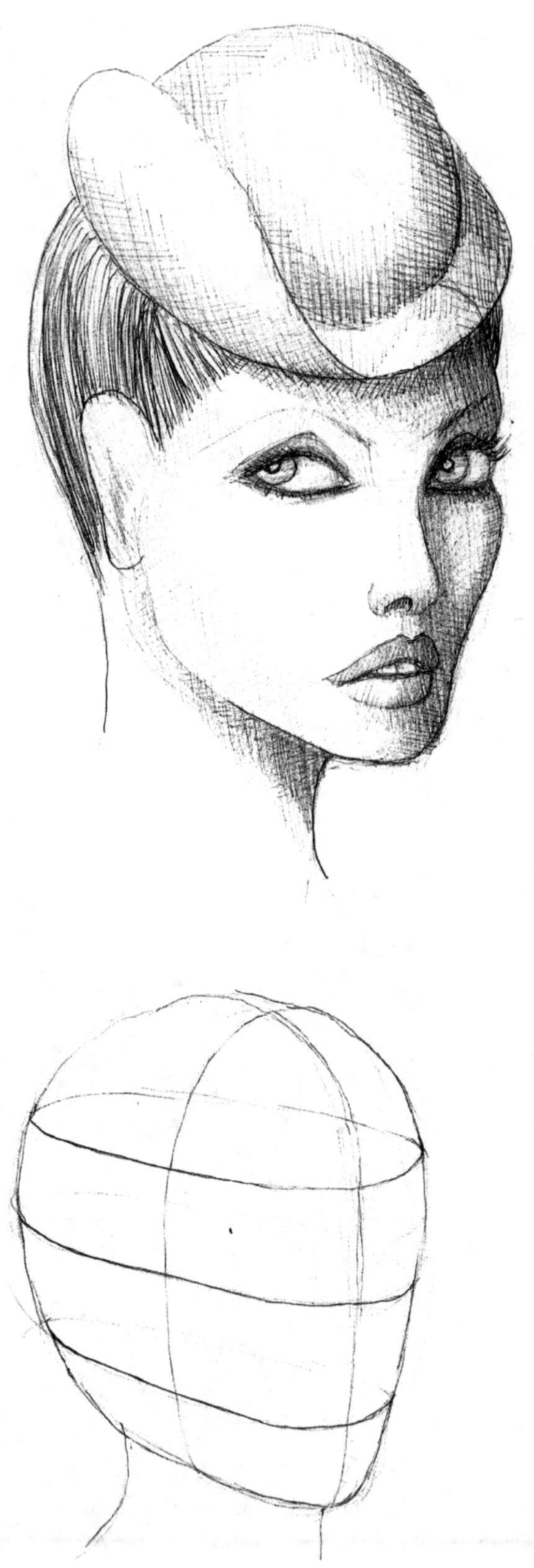

The quarter profile is the favorite of many artists, and it is used extensively in many drawings and paintings. It is easy to shade and highlight, and it gives the face a lot of dimension and depth. The profile is basically the shape of a lopsided egg. Instead of vertically dividing in half, put the vertical division on the side of the face instead of the center. Put the guidelines on one side of the face closer together, depending on which side of the profile you are doing. The horizontal divisions will remain the same.

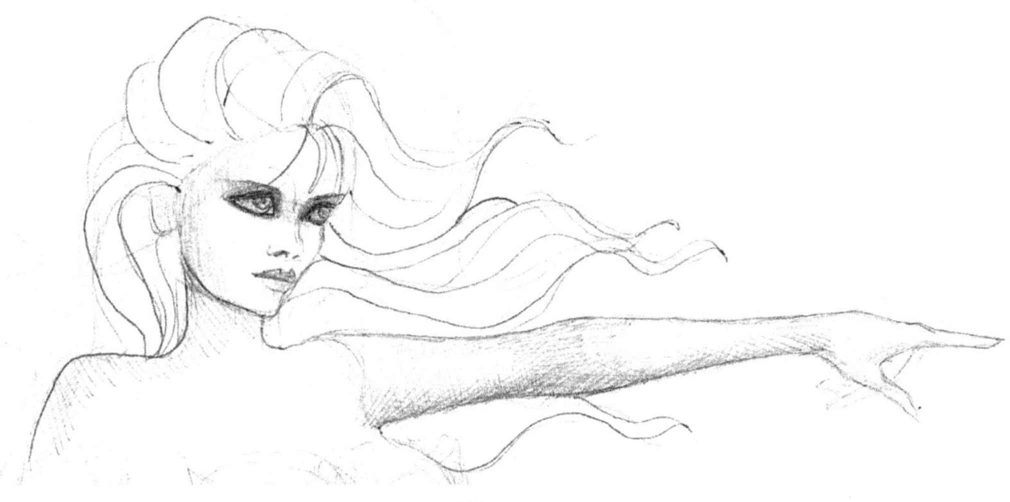

Quarter profile

Figure: 1

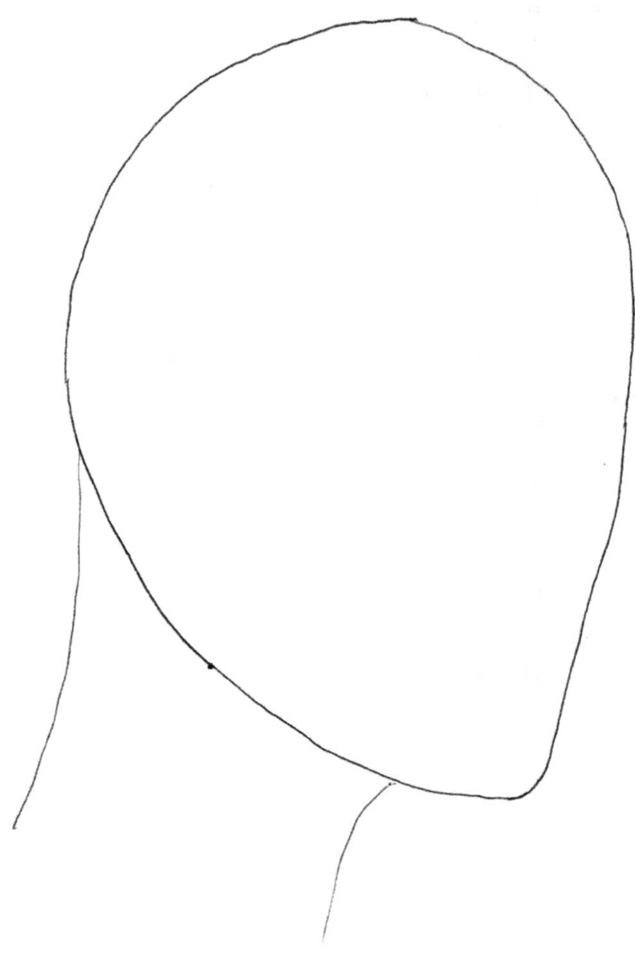

Draw the contour of a lopsided egg shape.

Figure: 2

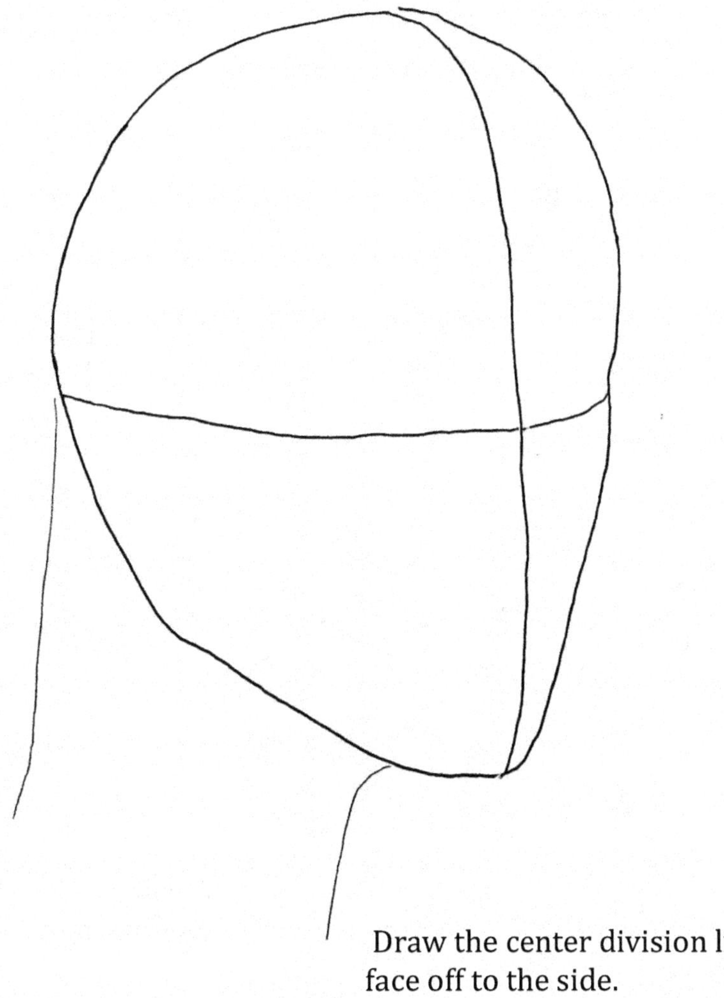

Draw the center division line of the face off to the side.

Figure: 3

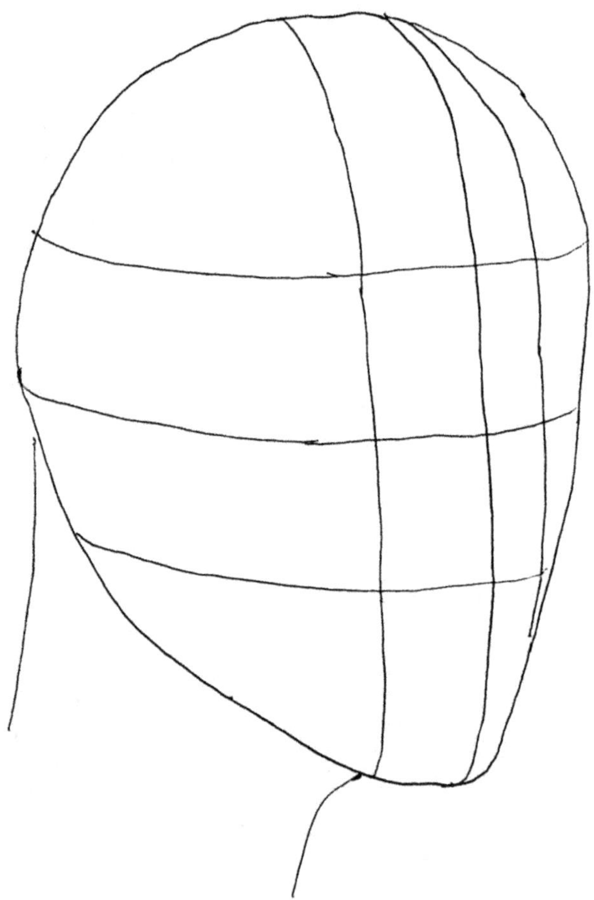

Divide the face into four quarters.

Figure: 4

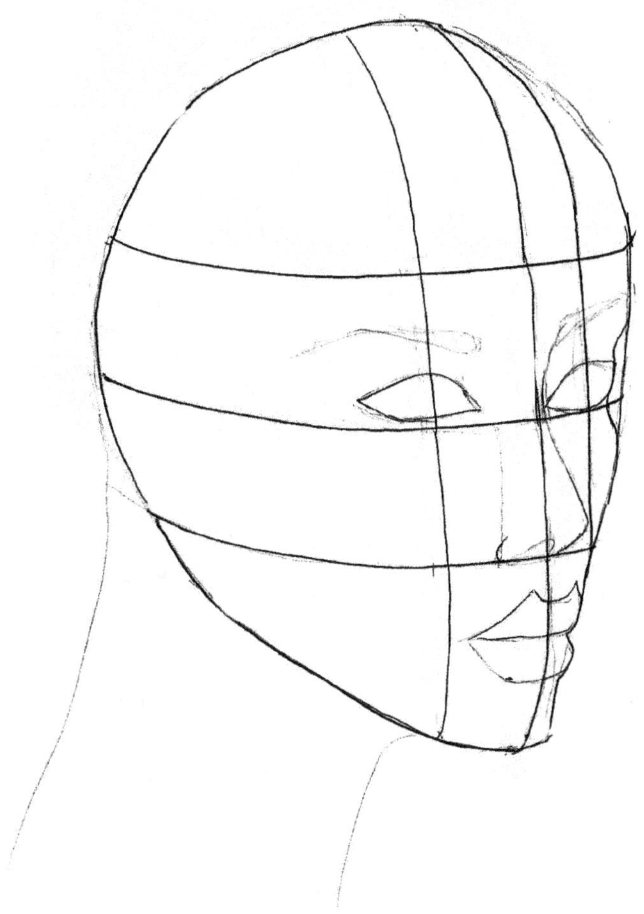

Draw in the face features.

Figure: 5

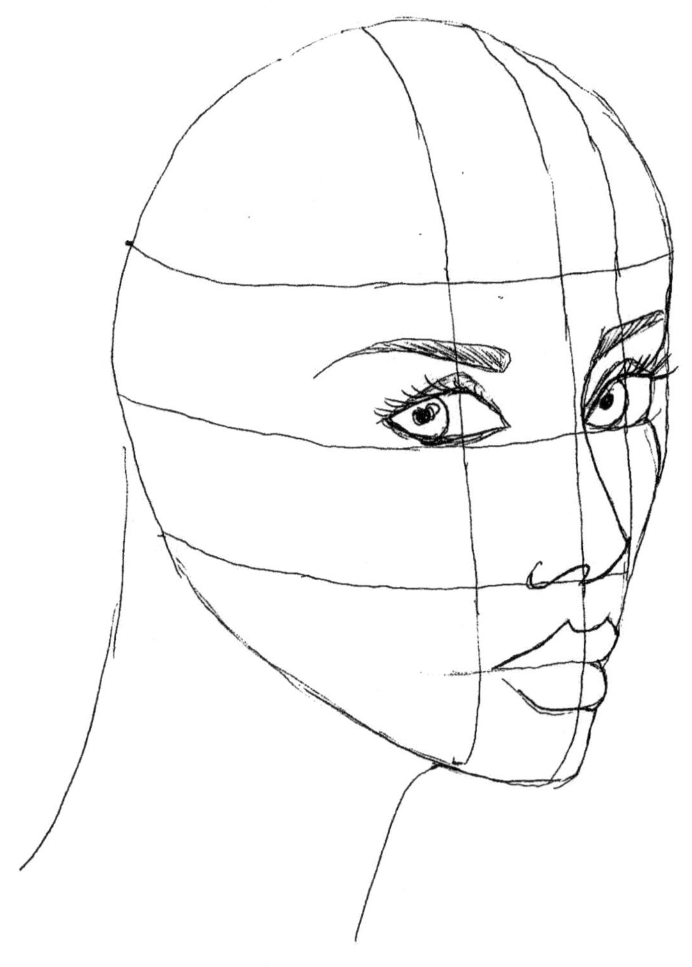

Figure: 6

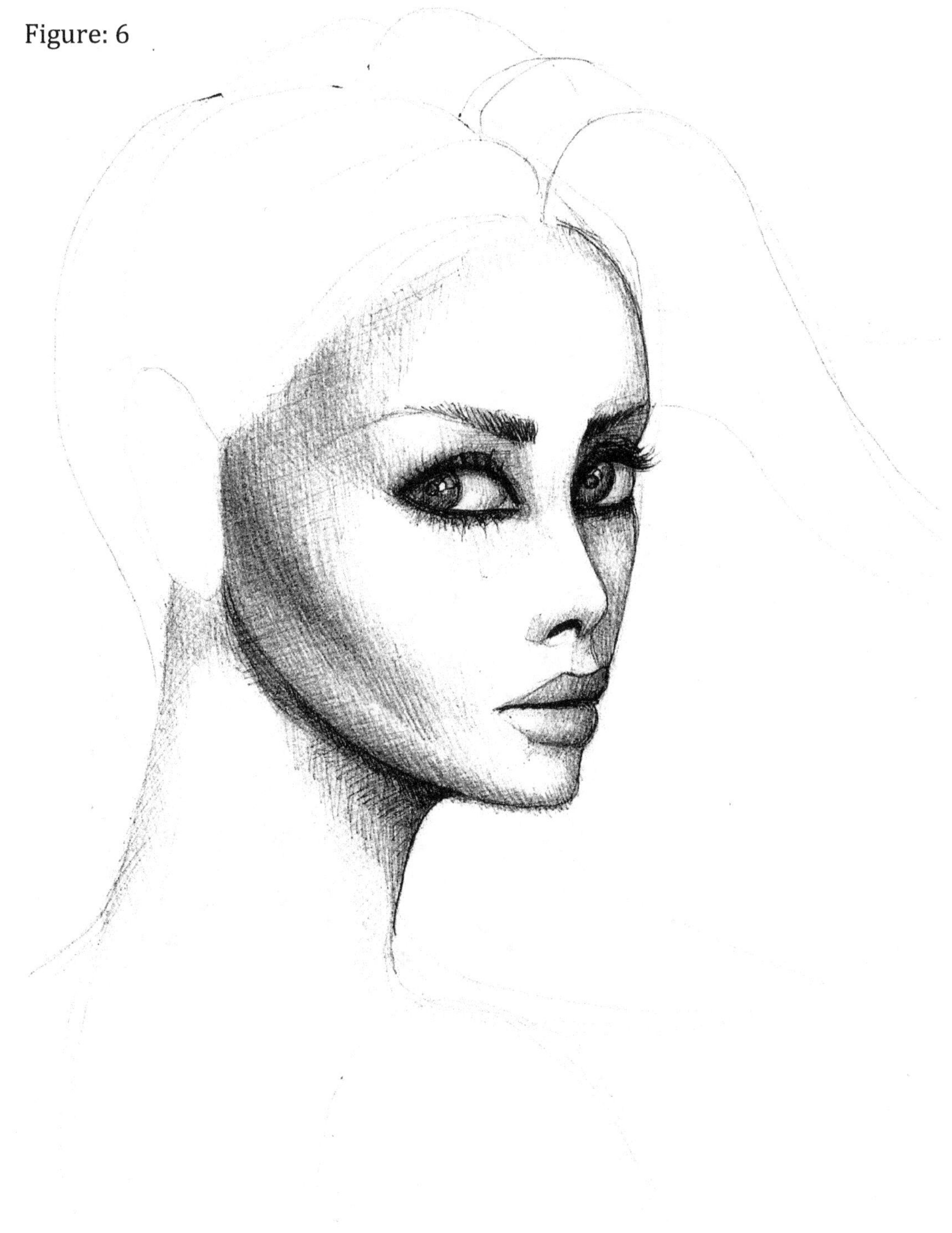

The full profile.

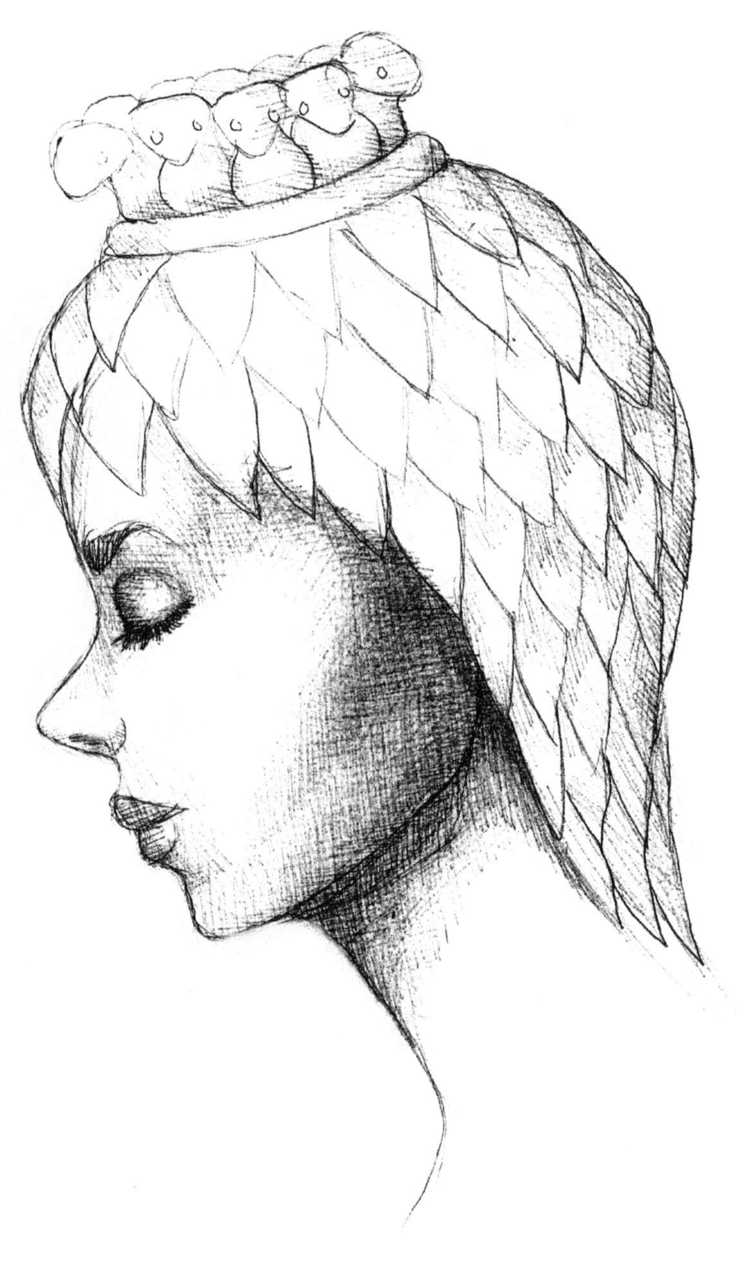

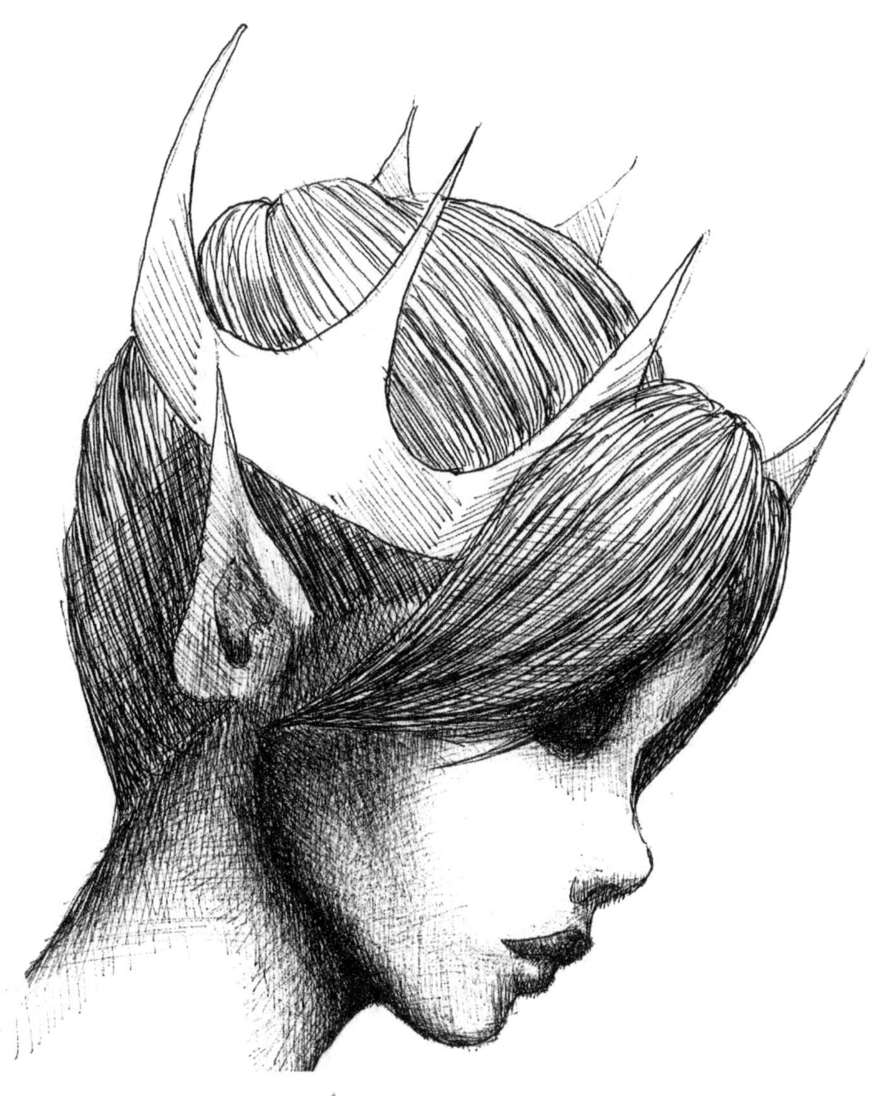

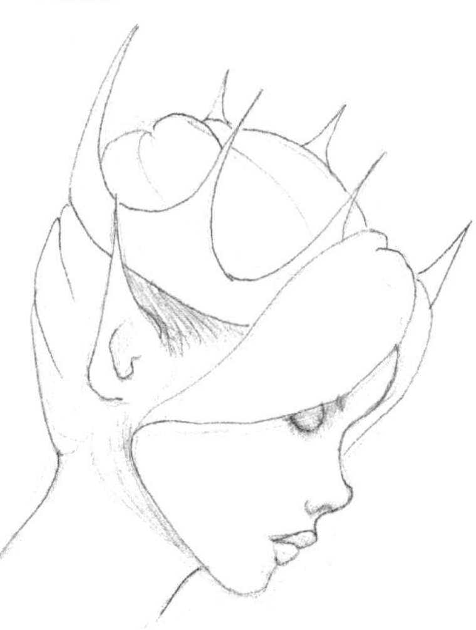

The full profile is one of the easiest to draw. This pose is ideal for showing the delicate and refined beauty of the female fantasy face. This pose can also be used to illustrate the regal and majestic qualities of the characters that come from faraway kingdoms. For example, the profile pose is perfect for displaying the pointed ears of an elf princess.

Figure: 1

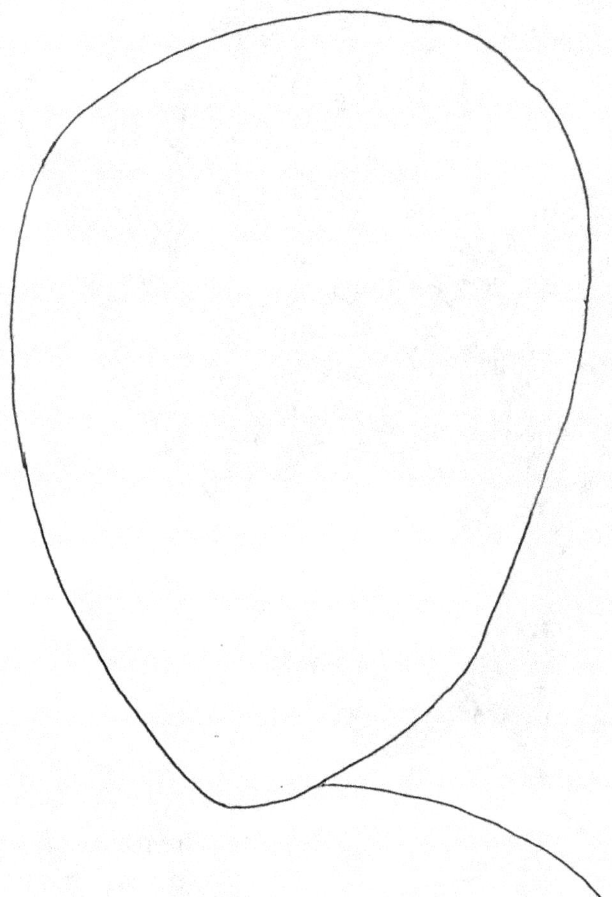

Draw the loop shaped egg.

Figure: 2

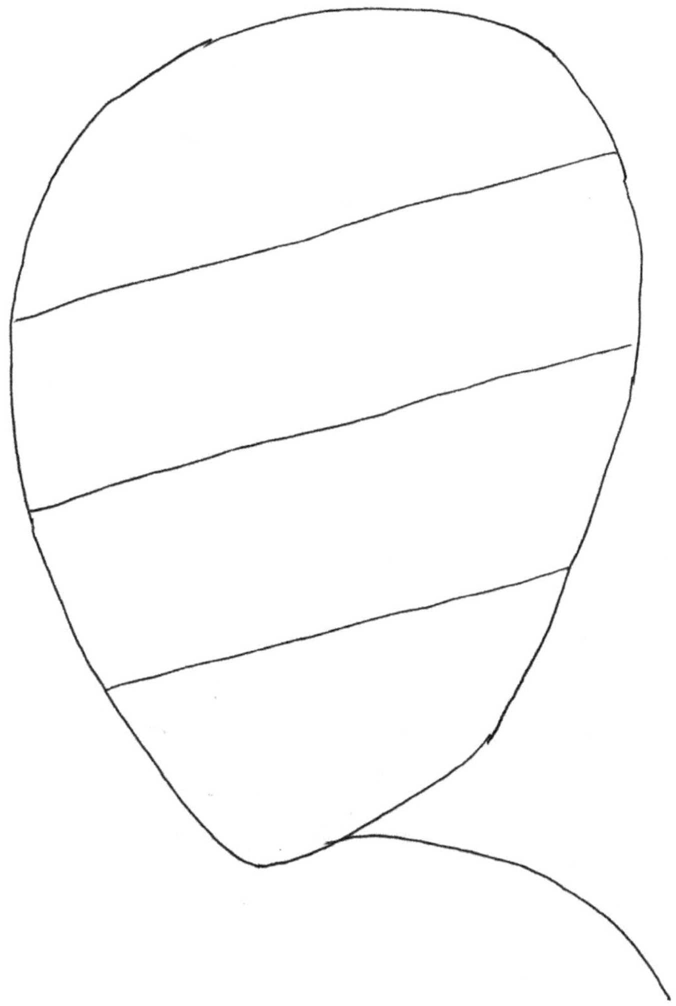

Divide the face into four parts. Angle the lines downward if the face will be looking down.

Figure: 3

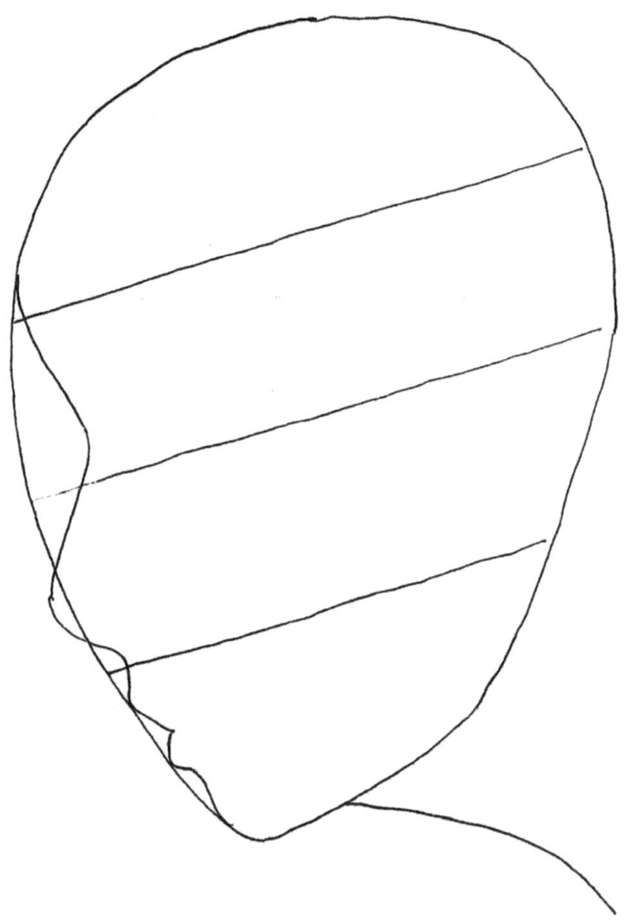

Draw the in the contour of the face. Put the bridge of nose on the centerline.

Figure: 4

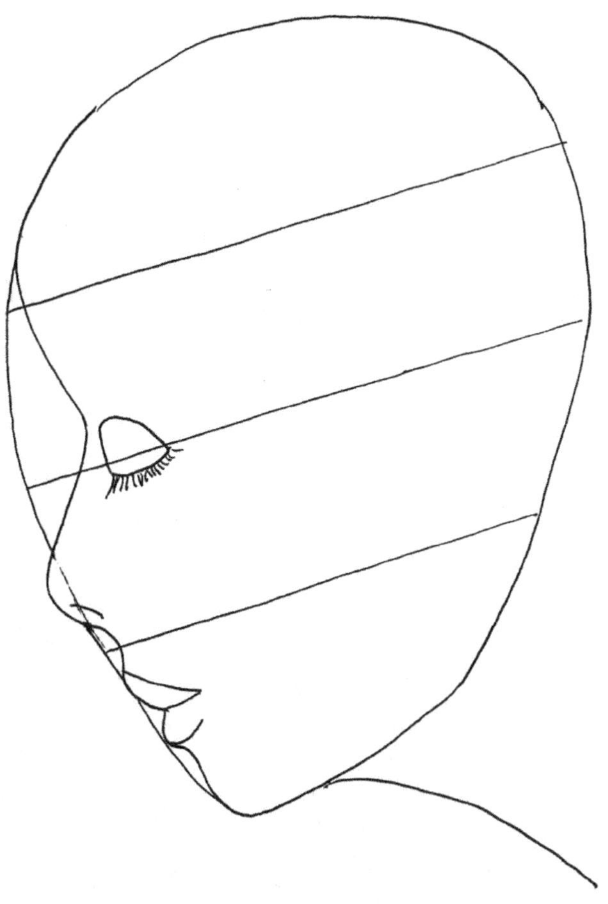

Draw in the features using the guidelines.

Figure: 5

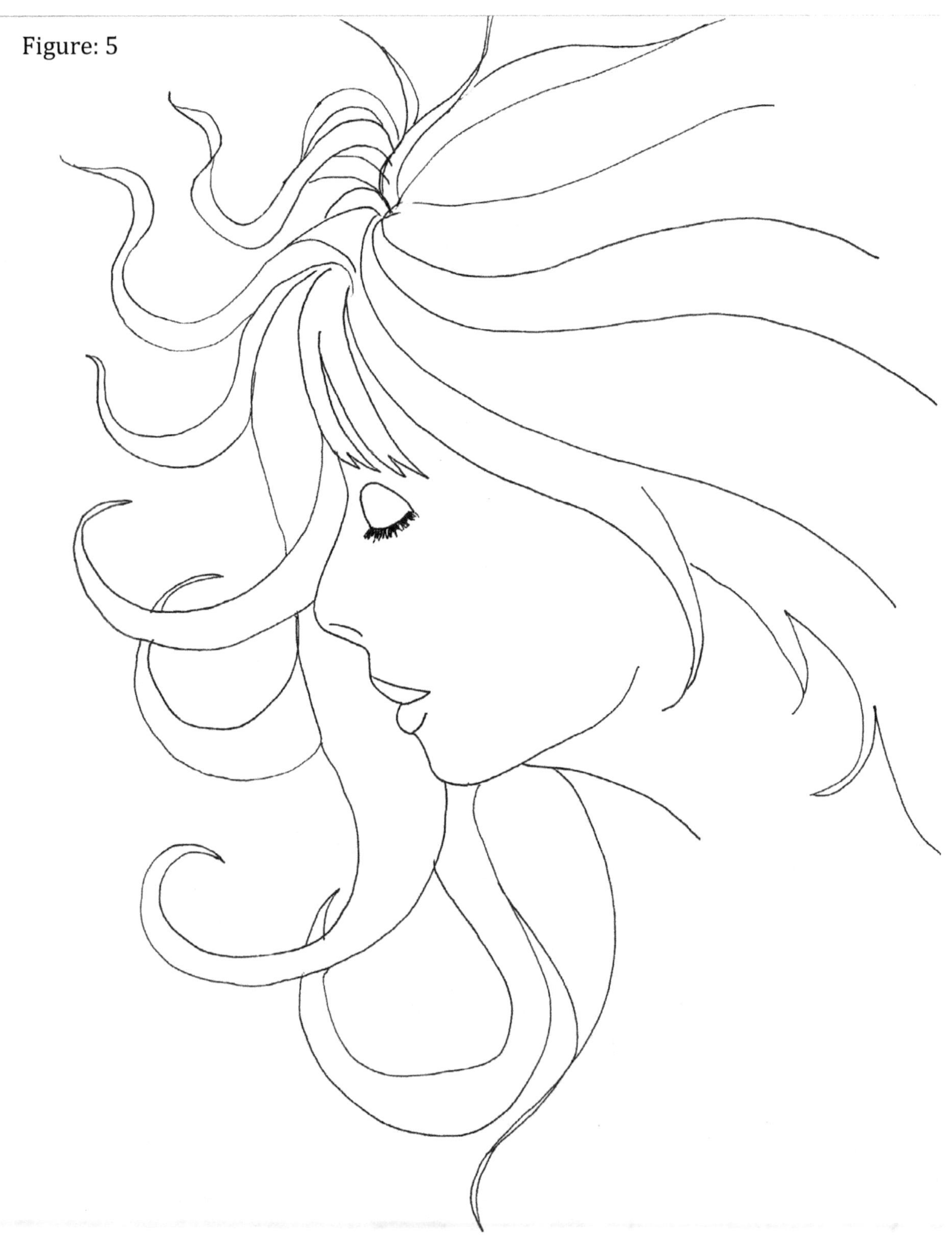

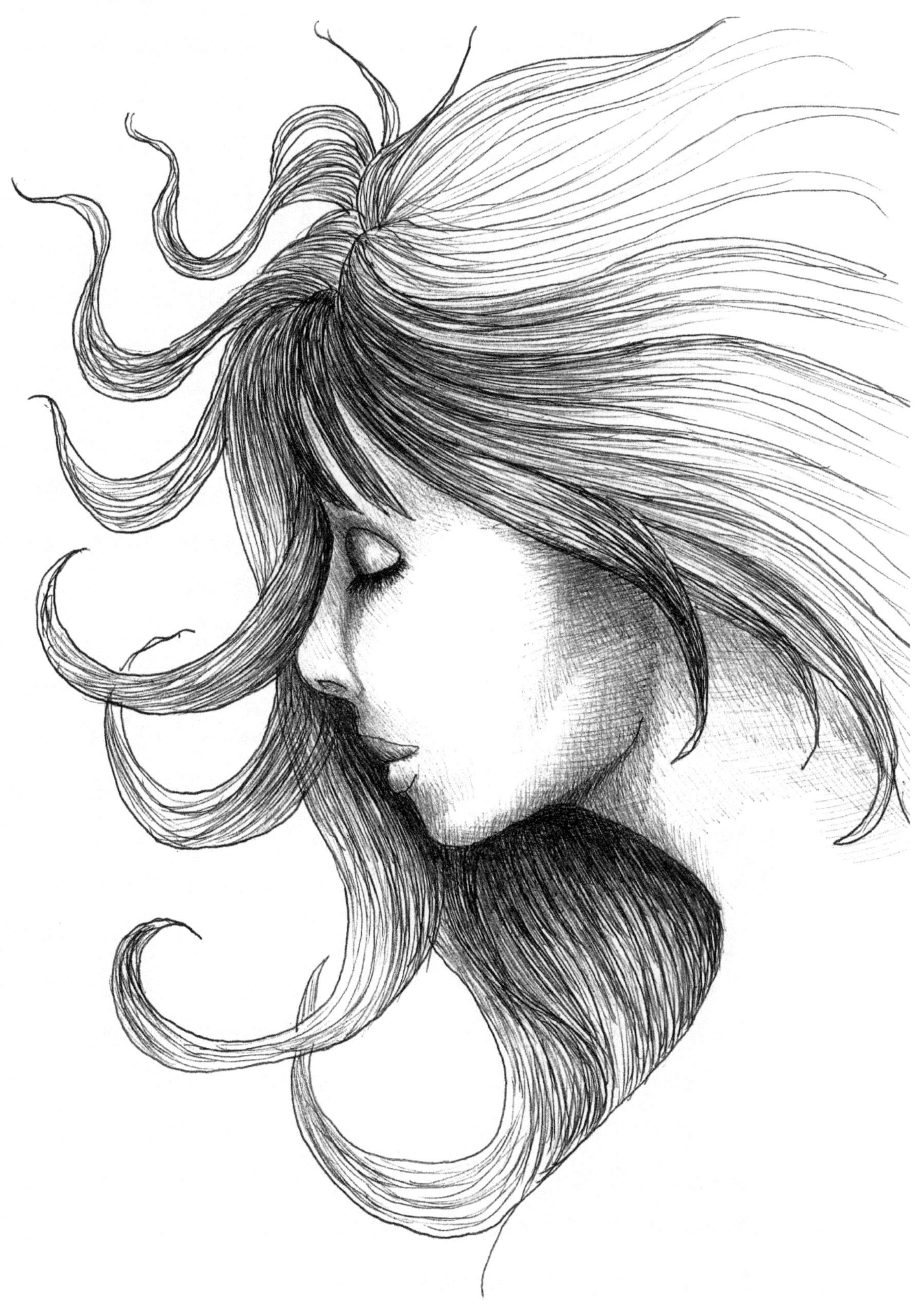

Chapter 4
Facial Features

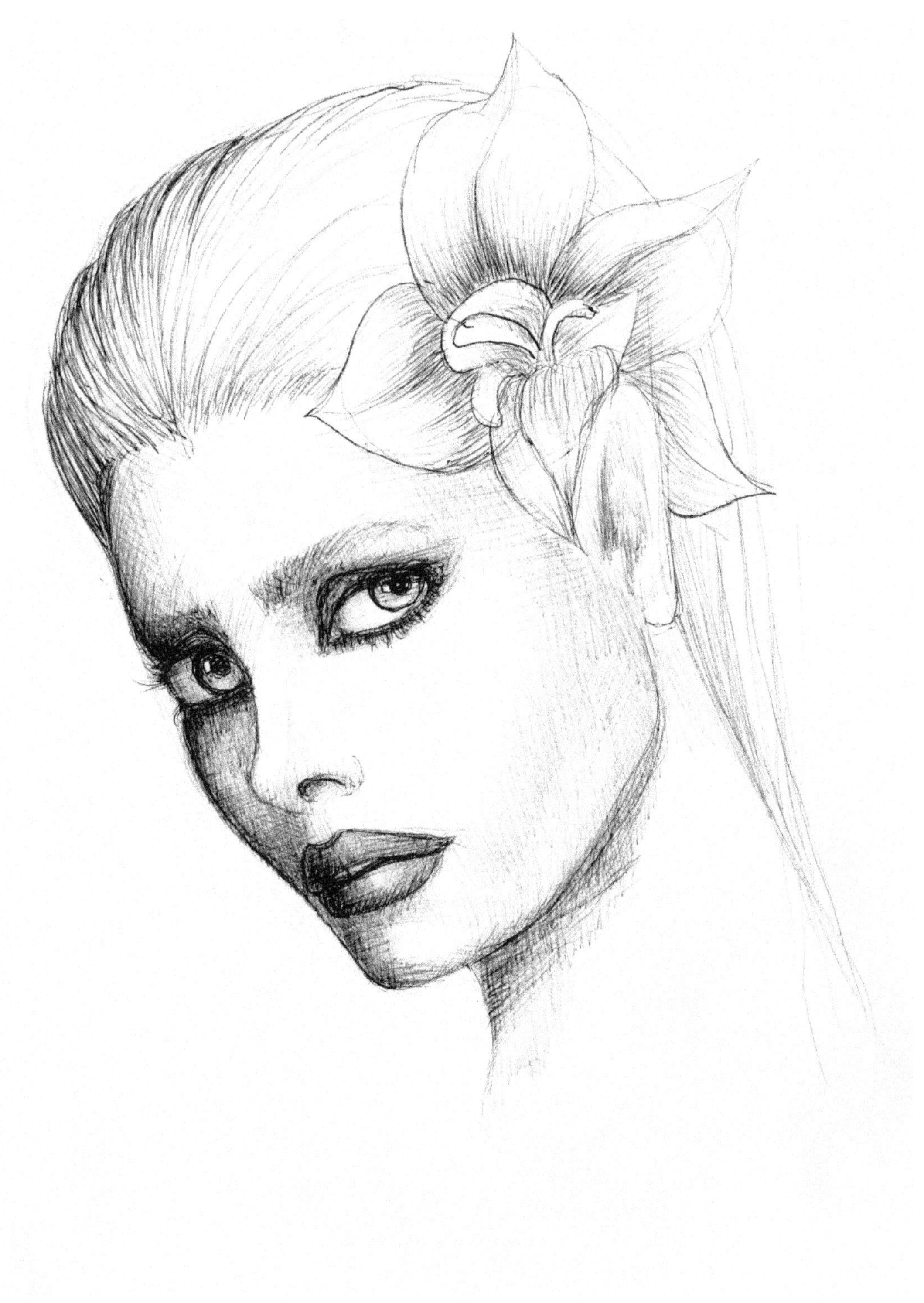

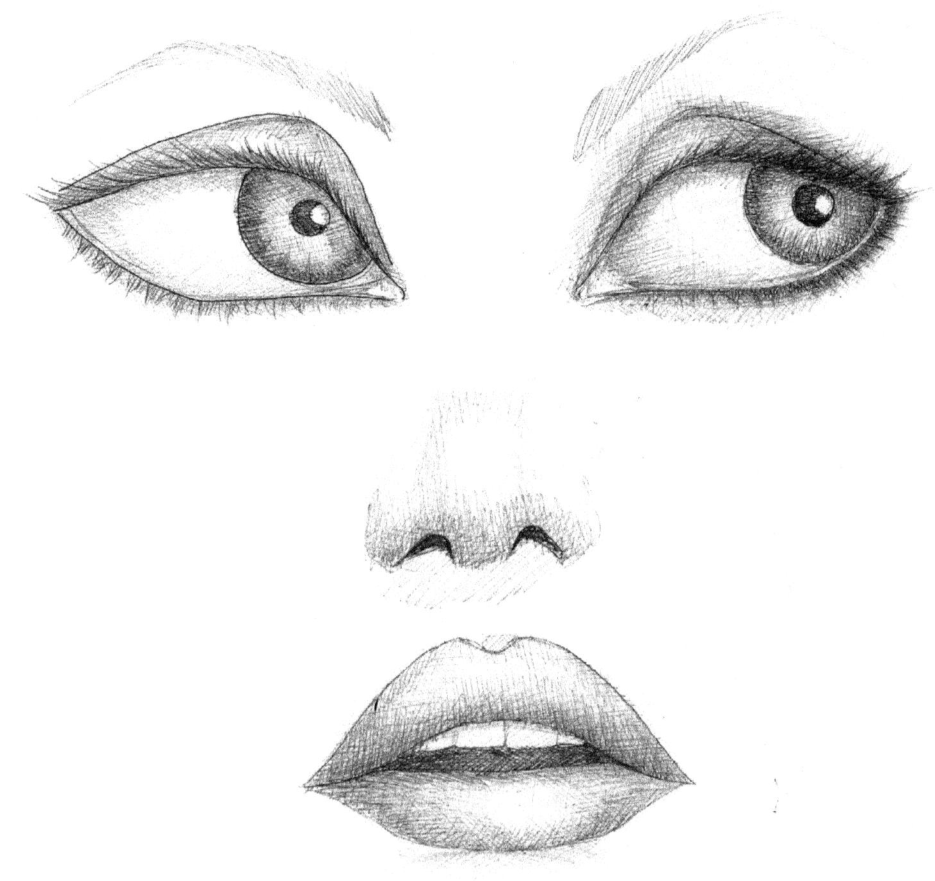

The facial features are what makes the female fantasy face look unique, and what gives it character. For example, you can make characters look innocent or evil by the shape and angle of their eyes. You can make the face look sad or mean by how you draw the mouth. The nose can be drawn very delicately or very strong in appearance.

When drawing the female fantasy face, keep in mind that you want to slightly accentuate the individual features. For instance, the whole eye area can be shaded in. The lips can be fully outlined. You can draw the nose extremely delicately or very defined. If the hair is long, you can show it flowing in the air.

Each of these features of the female fantasy face are very unique and individual in there own right. Therefor, it is critical that you familiarize yourself with each of these facial features. I recommend that you practice drawing each of these features separately.

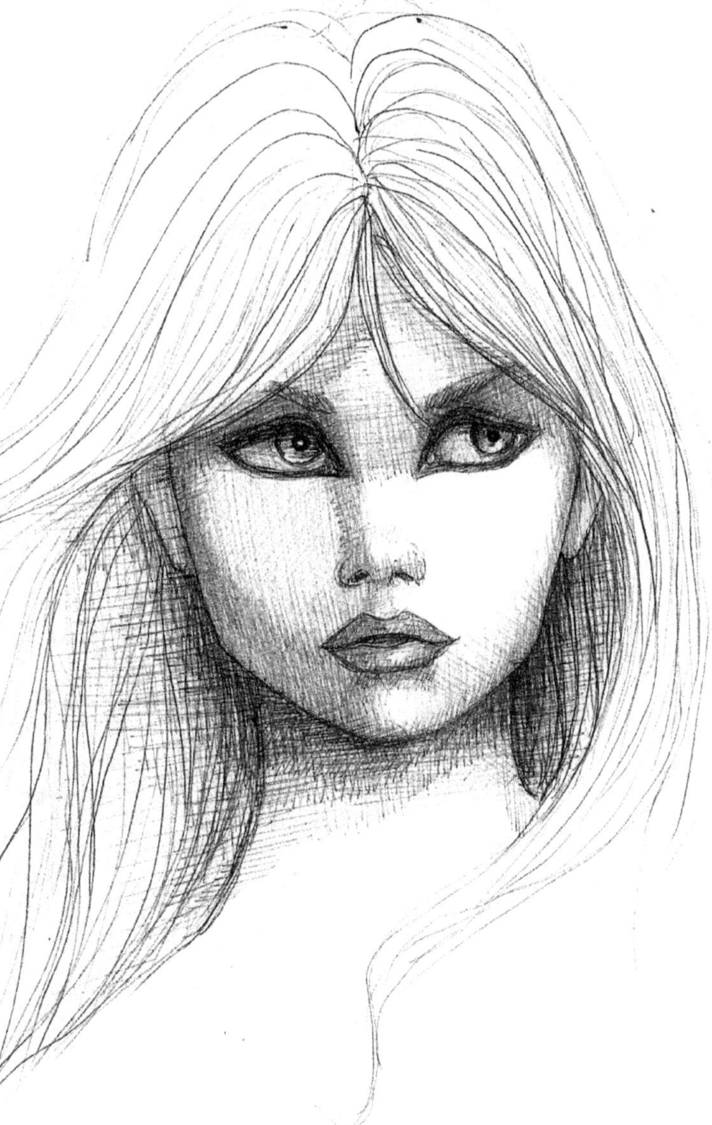

Drawing the eyes is my favorite part of the female fantasy face to draw. My objective is to draw them with a certain depth of expression. I strive to give them a look of intensity, and I always make them the focal point of the entire portrait.

I use extensive shading on the entire eye area including the actual eyeball. The eyes can be drawn to express many different emotions, moods, and feelings. The eyes are the most complex part of the face, and they are comprised of many different parts.

For instance, the eyeball alone contains many different parts, such as the sclera, iris, pupil, and the lens. In the outer eye we have the upper and lower eyelids, eyelashes, and the tear ducts.

I recommend you study and become very familiar with every part. Practice drawing the eyes by themselves, over and over, until you become an expert at doing them.

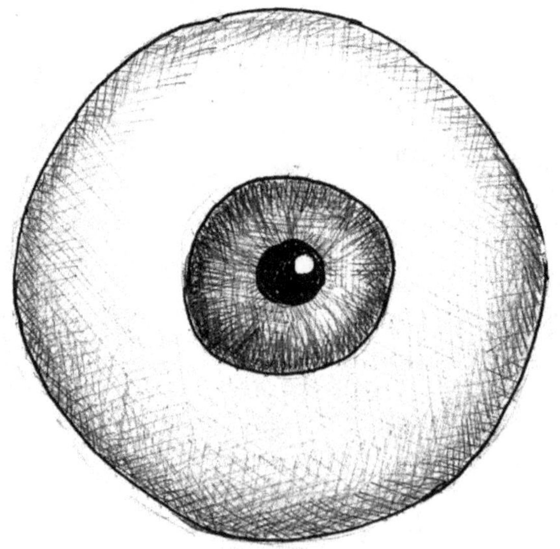

Drawing the eye

Draw the top arch first.

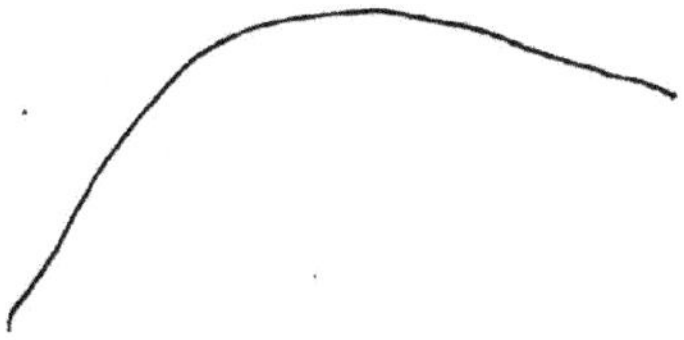

Add the bottom curve.

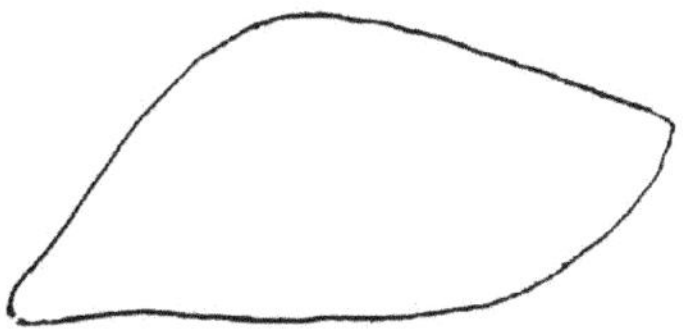

Draw the eyelid.

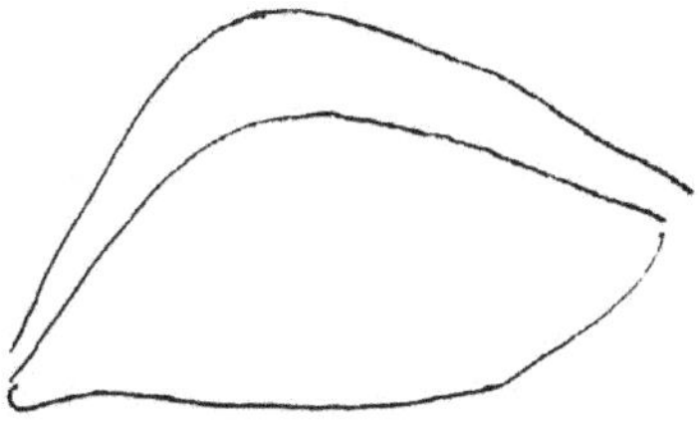

Draw the iris and the pupil.

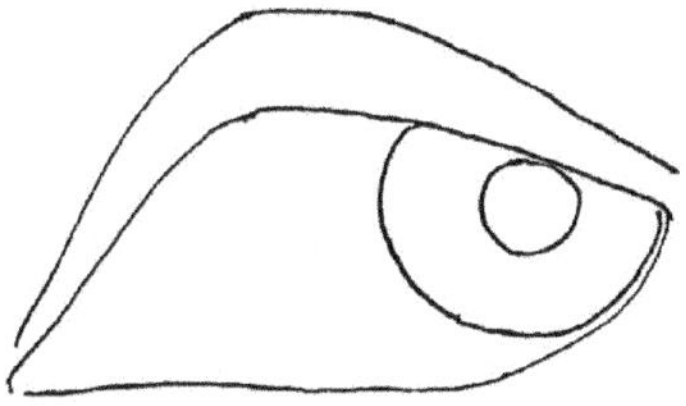

Now, add the lashes.

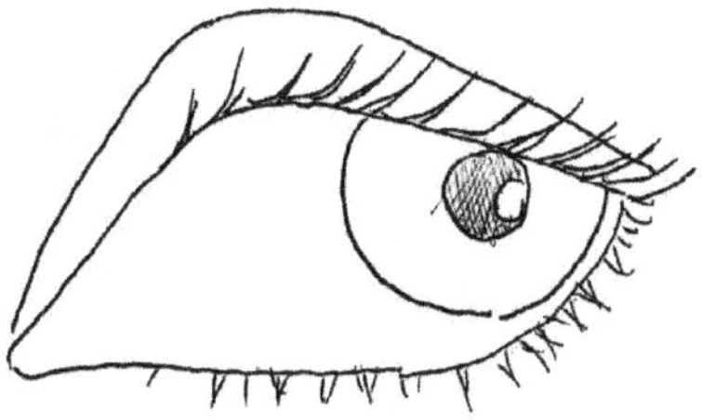

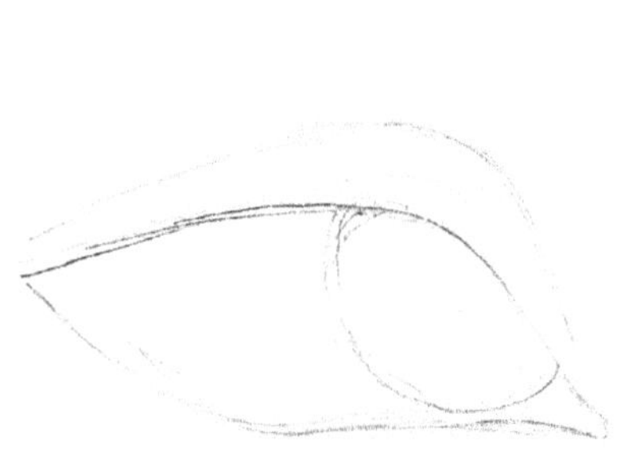
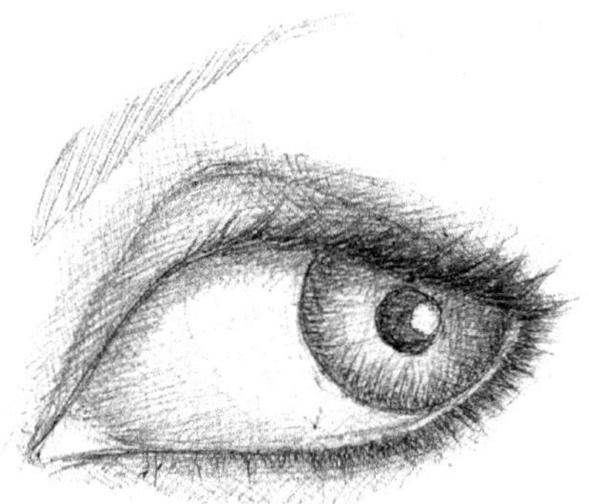

Eyes come in many different, sizes, styles, and shapes. Here are a few examples of the shapes I like to use.

This diagram shows the steps from left to right on how to create different types of eyes.

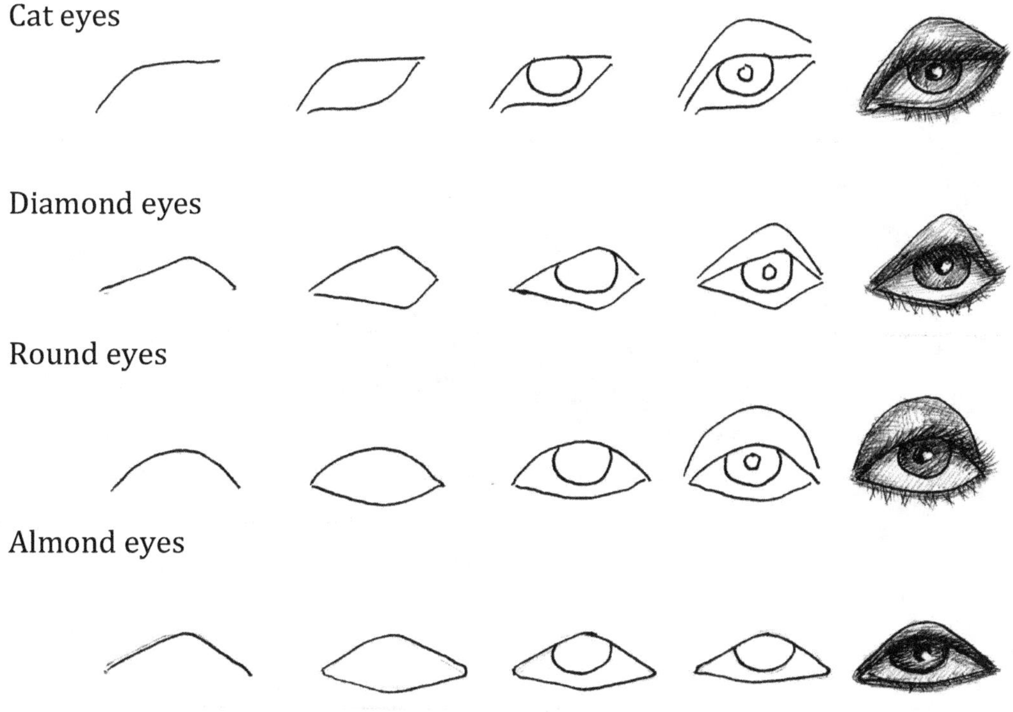

These are just a few of the types of eyes you can do. Practice drawing and creating your own type of eyes.

Drawing the lips

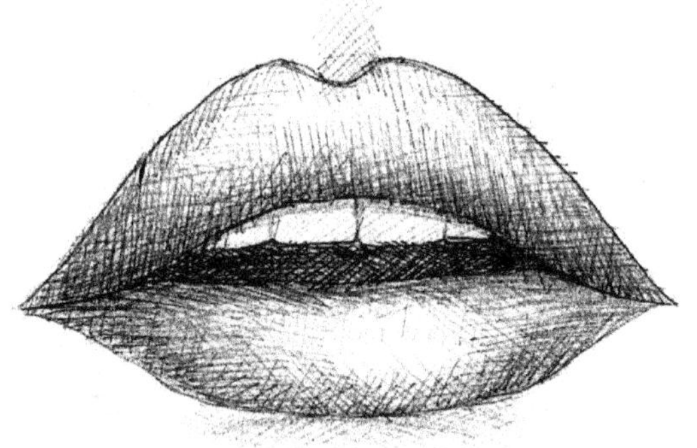

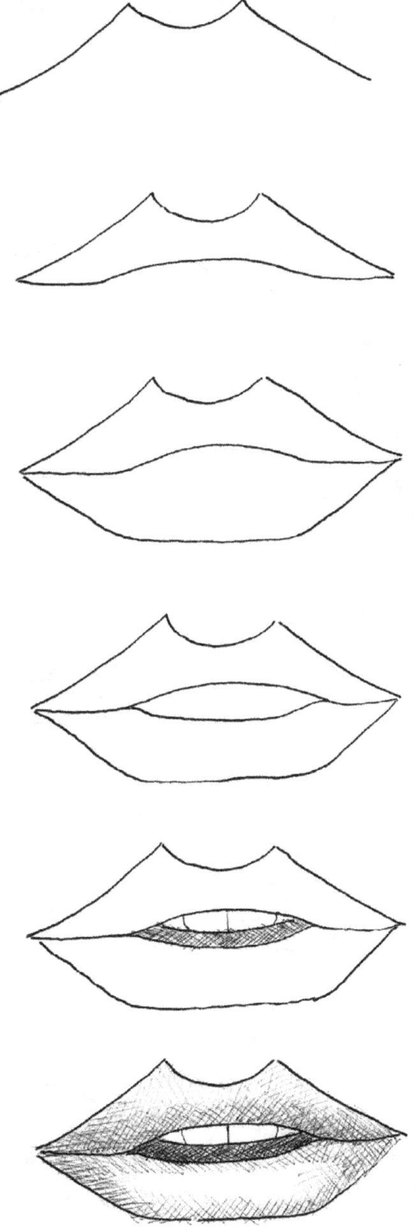

When you have completed drawing the lips, shade in the top first then the bottom. Shade in the lower portion of the top lip, then gradually move up the shaded area. Do the same with the lower portion of the lip.

Variation of lip styles

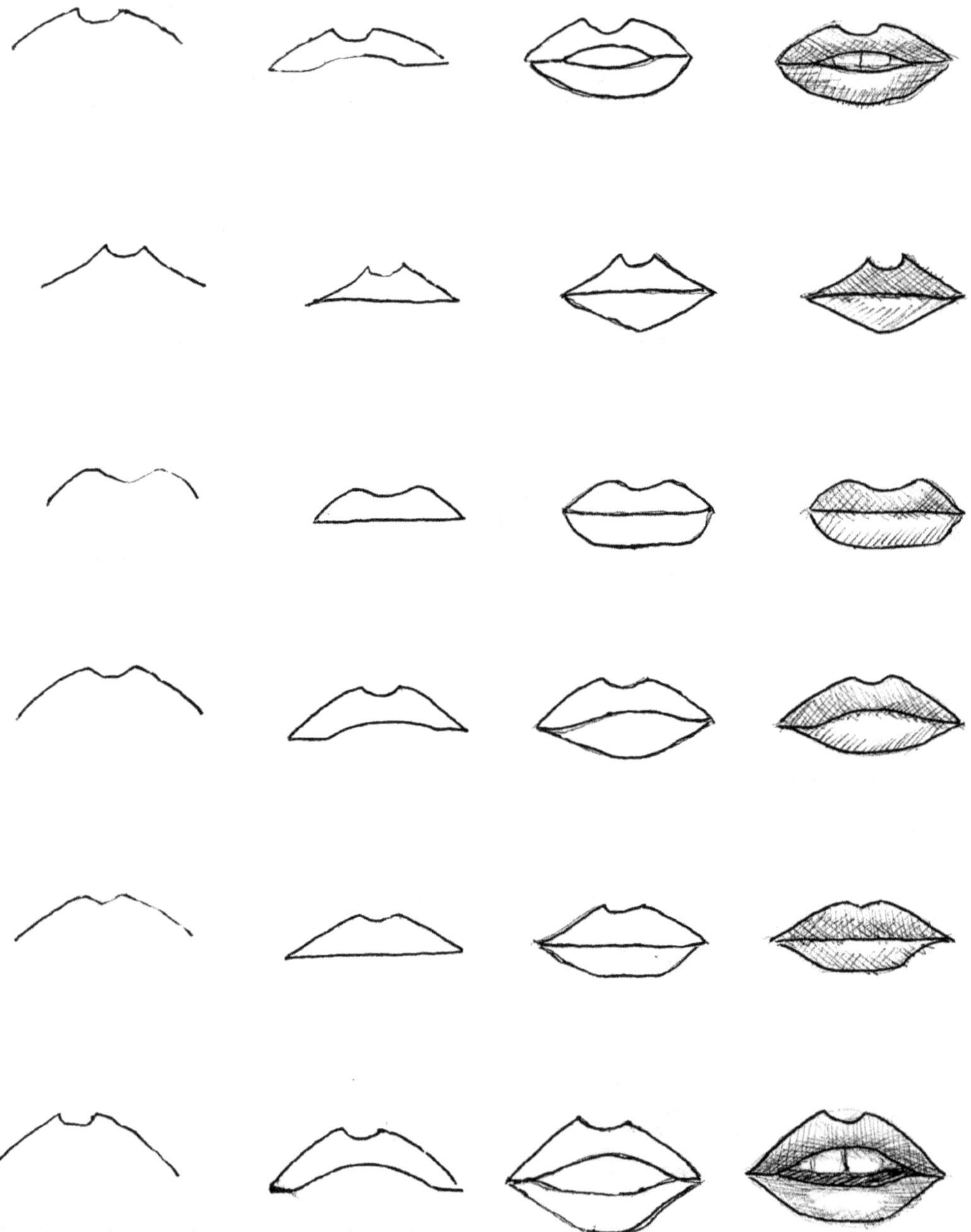

Drawing the nose

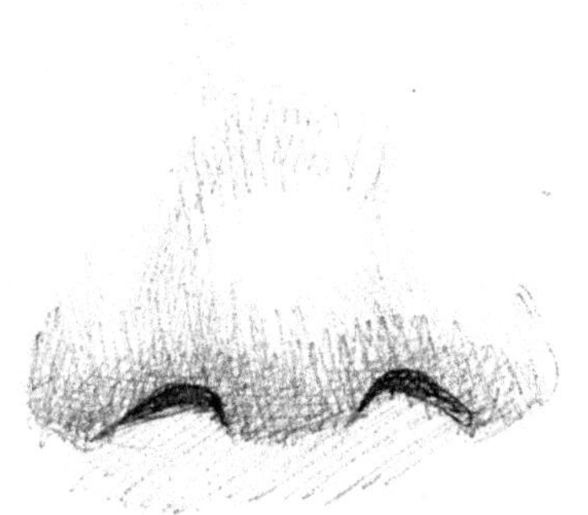

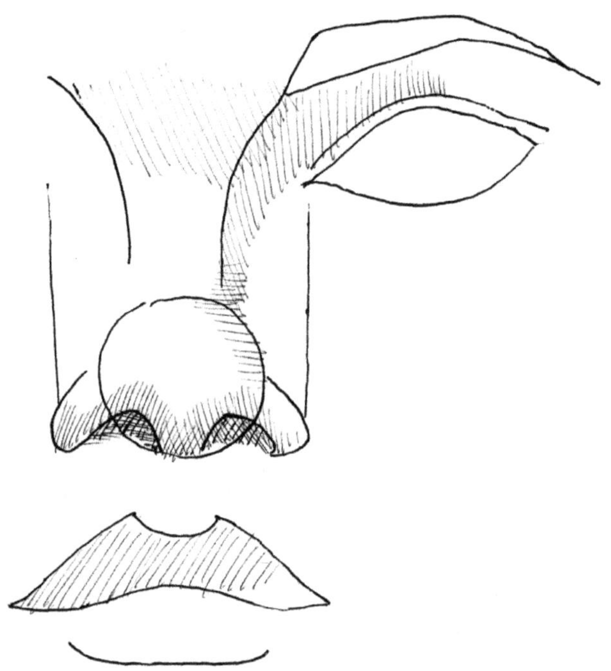

Draw the nose as delicately as possible. Try not to over shade the nose, the less you draw of it the better. Keep most of the shaded area to one side. Then delicately shade in the nostrils, and the angles of the nose.

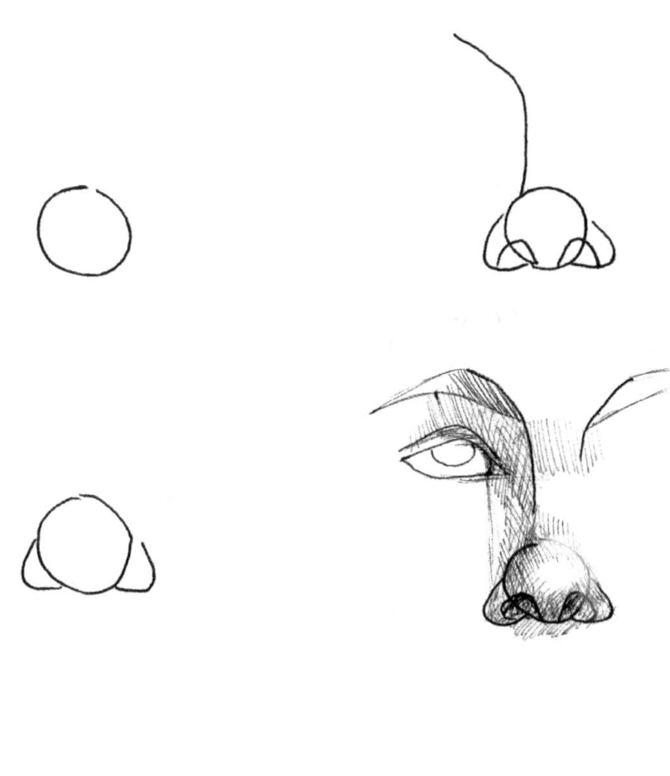

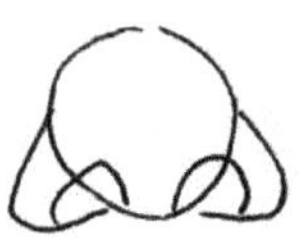

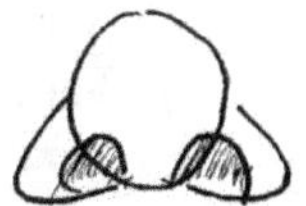

Drawing the hair

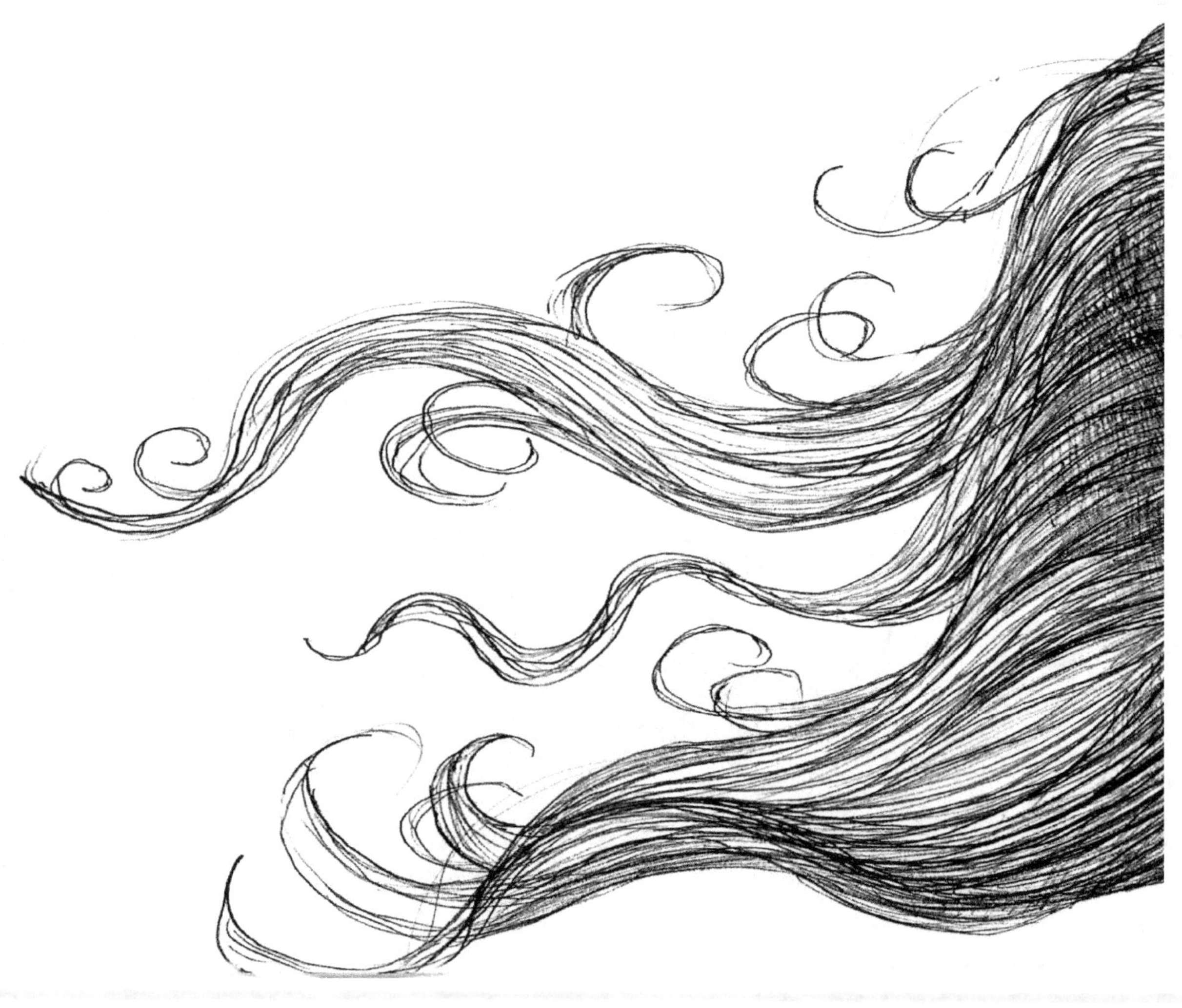

The hair on fantasy females is always a bit on the long side, and always flowing in the breeze. Drawing the hair can be one of the easiest parts to draw, it can also be the easiest to get wrong. If the hair is done wrong it can ruin the whole drawing. That is why I always draw the hair one section at a time. The reason I draw the hair section by section is because it can be very boring and redundant. So, I draw one part, then come back later and draw another section.

Figure: 1

Outline the entire hair area.

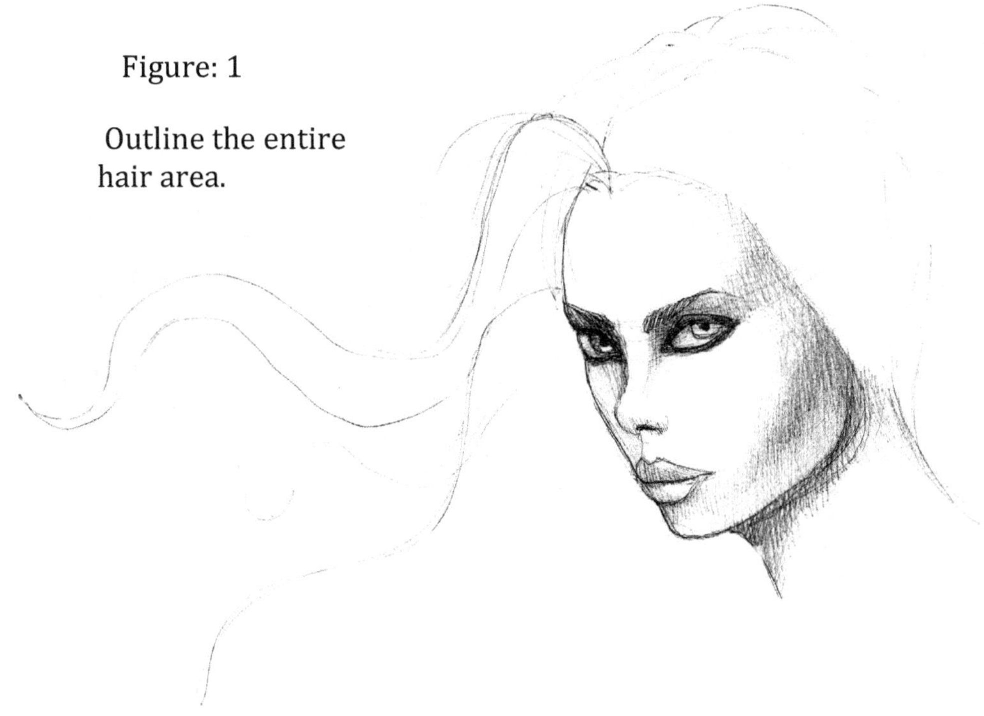

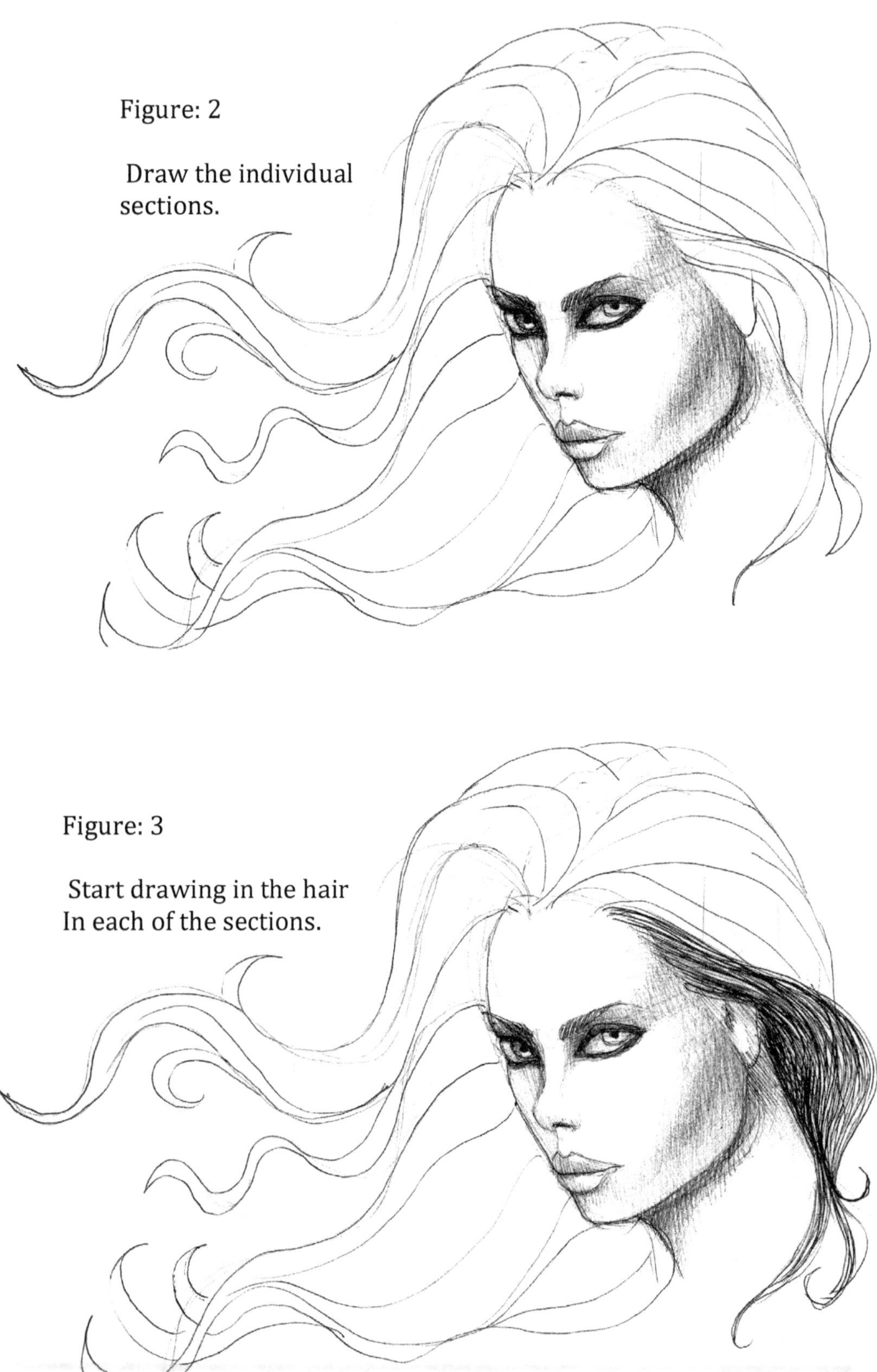

Figure: 2

Draw the individual sections.

Figure: 3

Start drawing in the hair In each of the sections.

Figure: 4

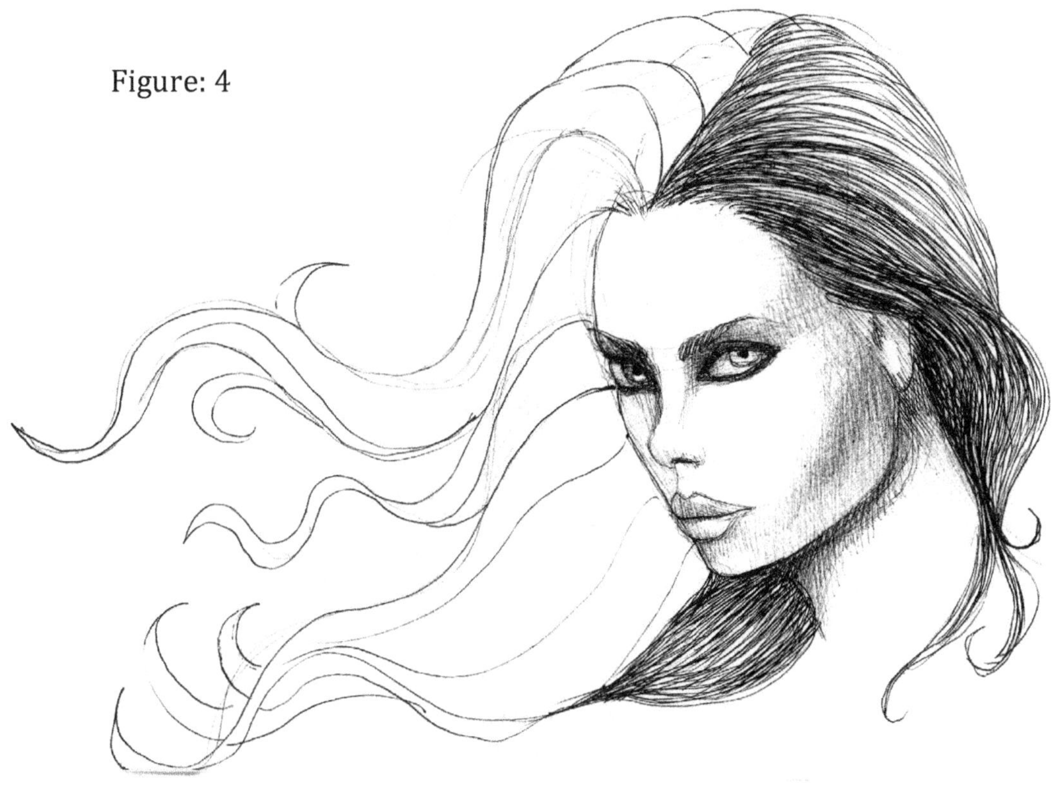

Figure: 5

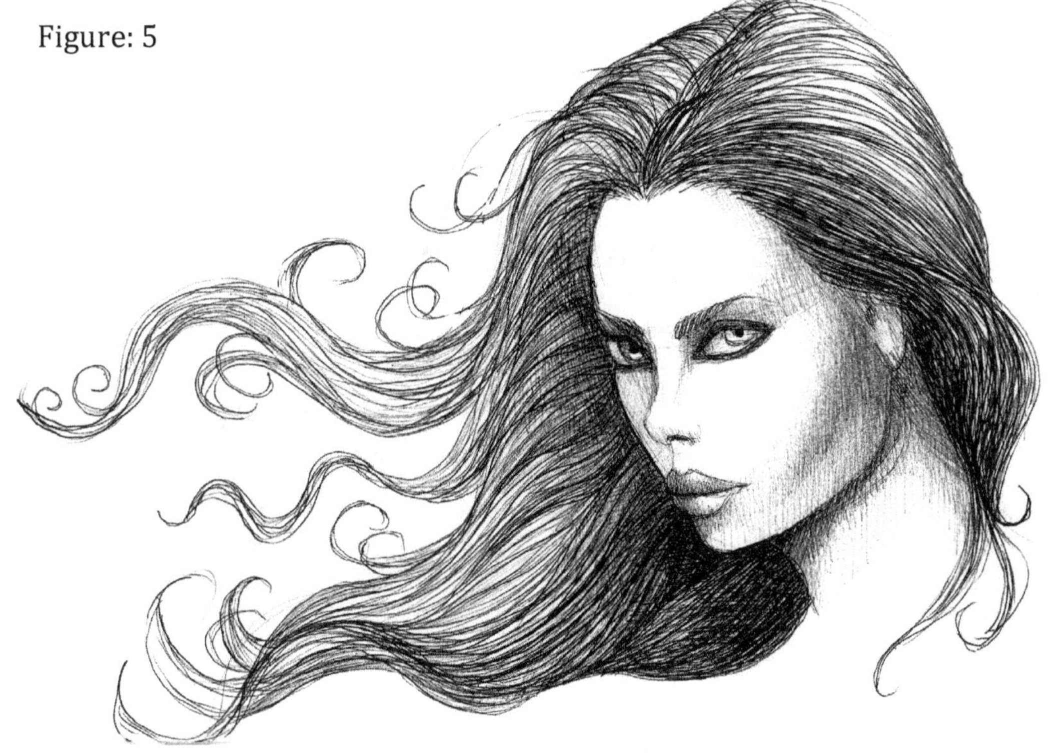

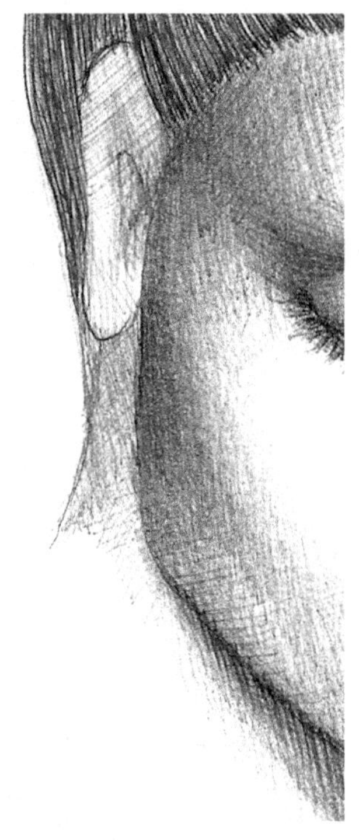

Drawing the ear

The ear is just a basic loop. Place the ear between the bottom of the nose and top of the brow.

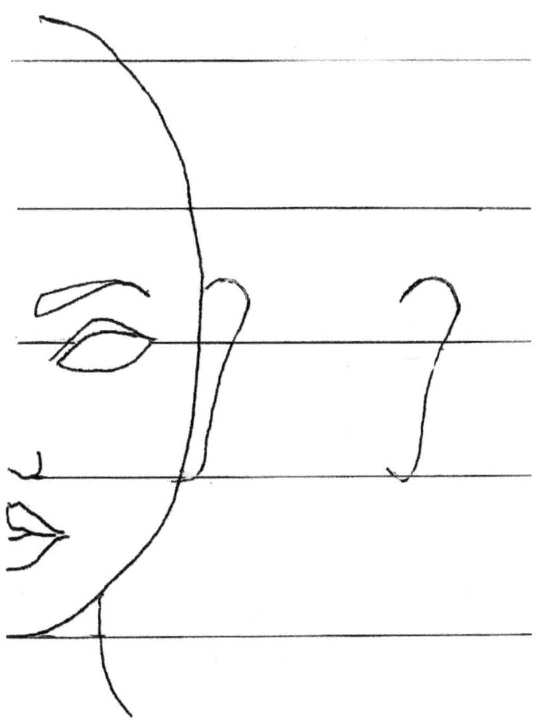

The side view of the ear is drawn by making a wider loop. Place the ear between the bottom of the nose and top of the brow.

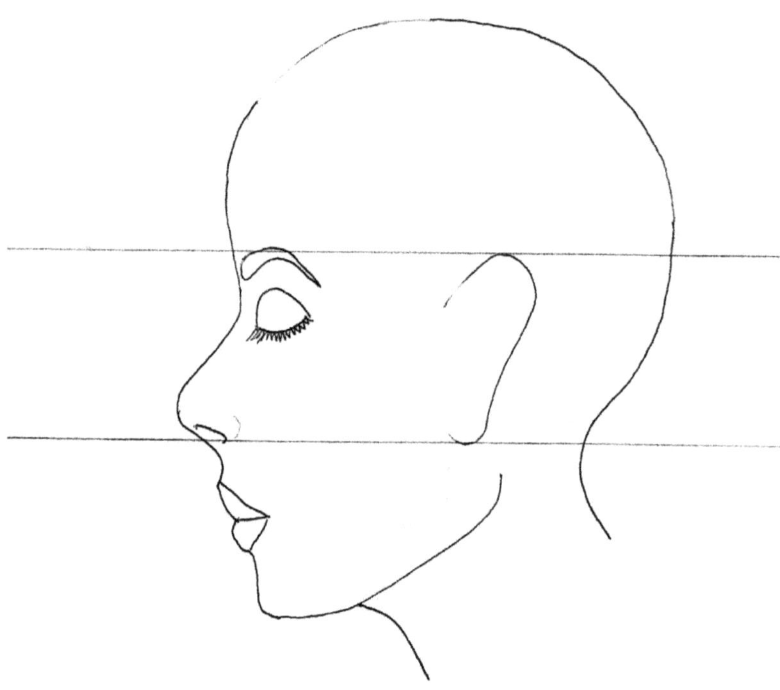

When drawing the shading of the rings inside the ear keep it simple and delicate.

Drawing fairy and elf ears.

When drawing elf or fairy ears, simply make the ears pointed. You can extend the ears as much. as you like.

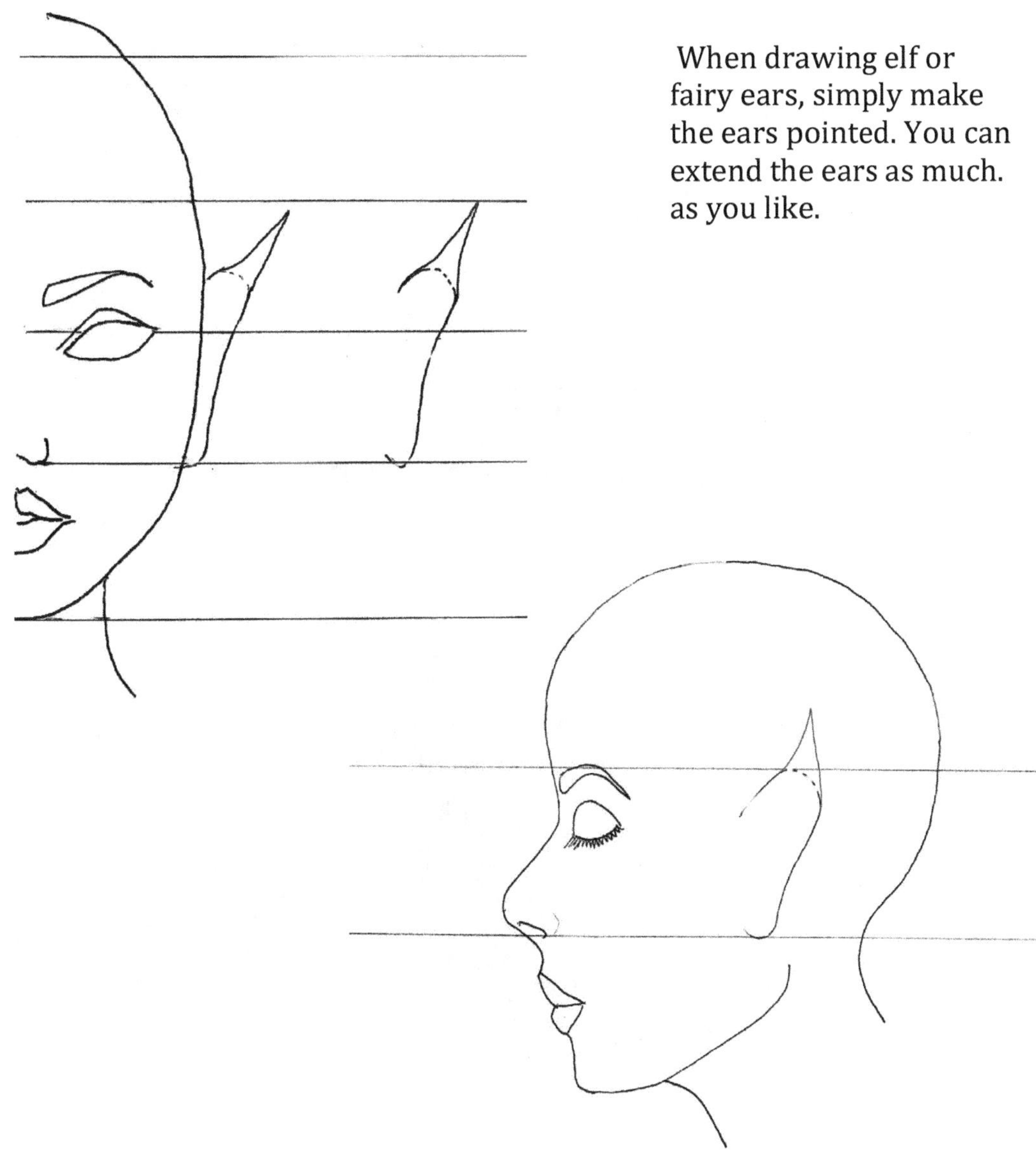

Chapter 5
Shading in the face

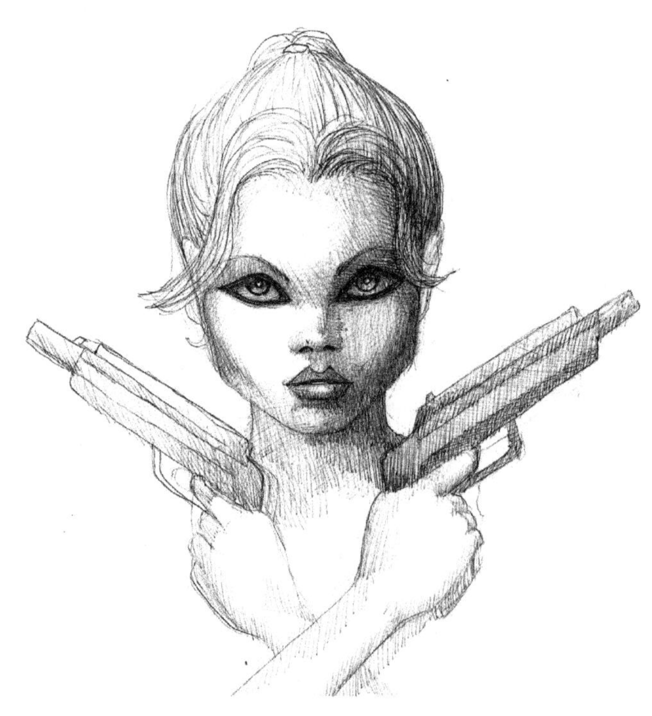

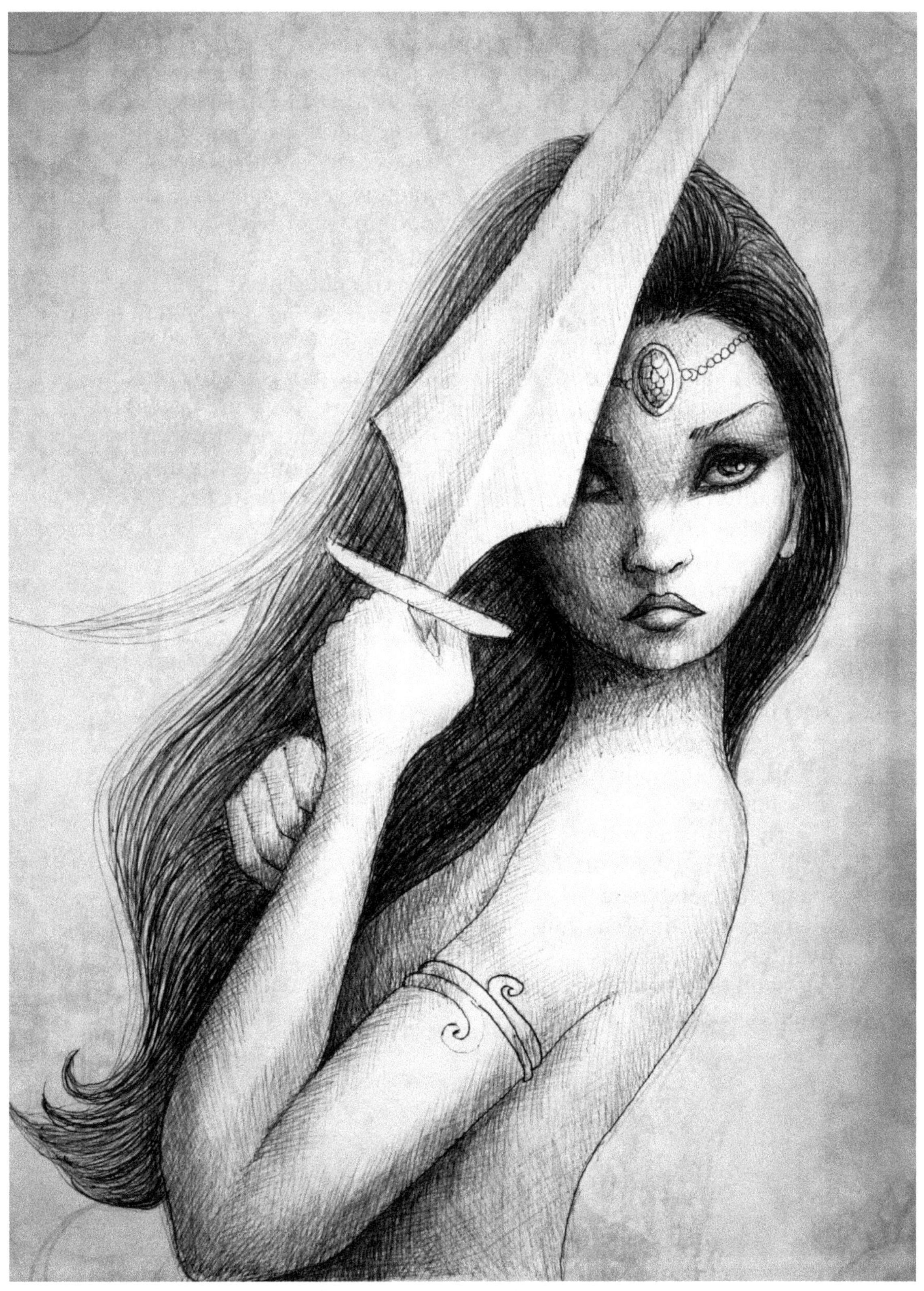

The final stage in drawing is shading everything in. At this stage make sure your drawing is just the way that you want it to be. If you can make any corrections or adjustments, do them now. Then determine the direction of the light source, and start the shading process.

- Start the shading with a general shading of the entire drawing. Lightly shade all the areas that you will be working on.
- Secondly, concentrate on the darker areas of the drawing. These are the parts of the drawing that you want to have some depth.
- Now, you can work on the specific areas of the drawing. Concentrate your shading on the individual face features.
- Lastly, go in and refine your shading. Work on the parts that need to be defined, and the areas you want to stand out. Also, work on the areas that you want the darkest.

Take as much time as you want when you are in the shading stage of your drawing. Be careful not to over shade everything. After each stage of the shading sit back, and examine your progress. Before continuing assess what areas require more work, and what areas do not. This is the final stage of your drawing, give it all that you have.

Also, it is important to note that this process does not have to be followed in the order that it is listed. For example, the detail shading can be done first.

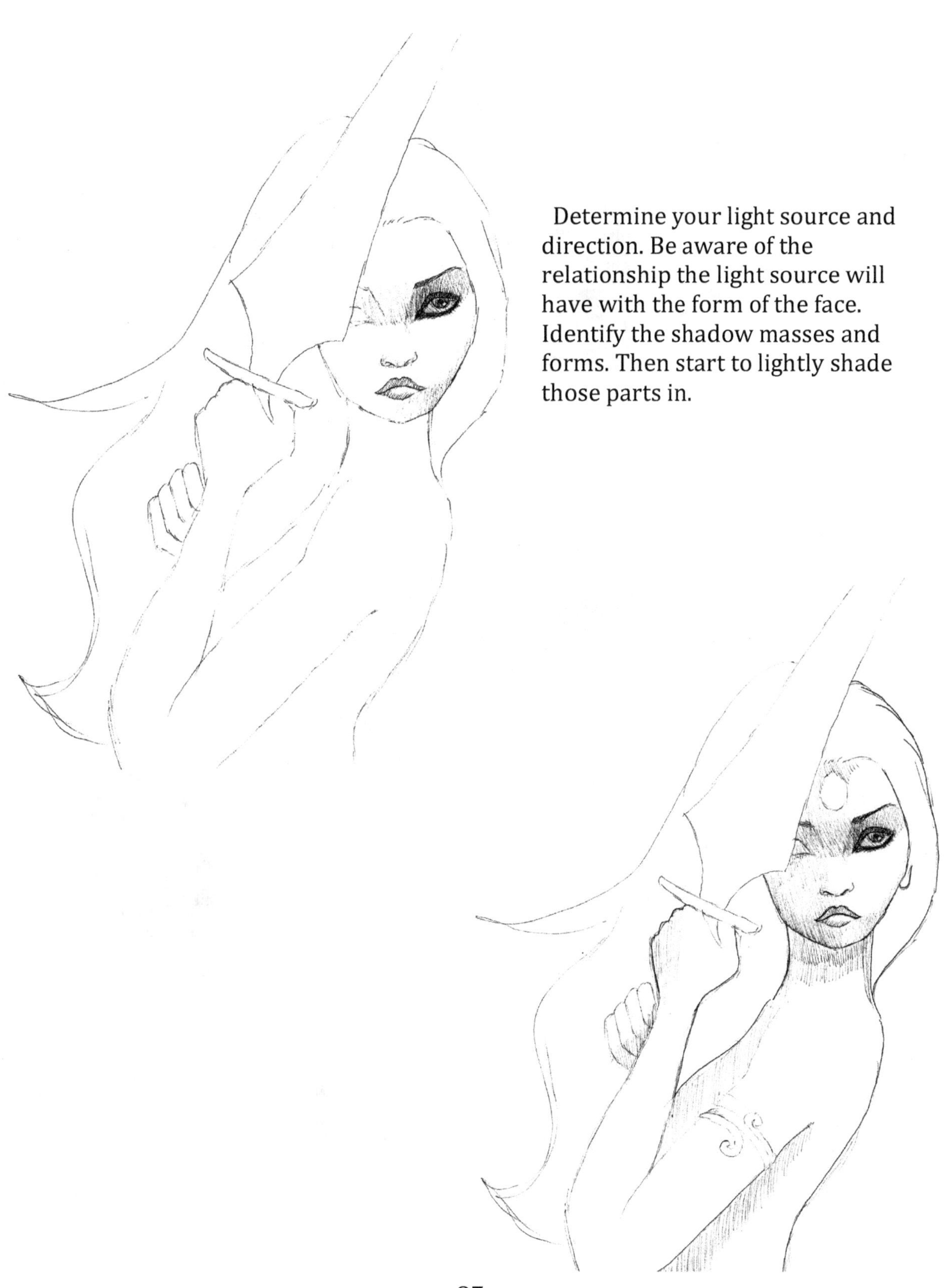

Determine your light source and direction. Be aware of the relationship the light source will have with the form of the face. Identify the shadow masses and forms. Then start to lightly shade those parts in.

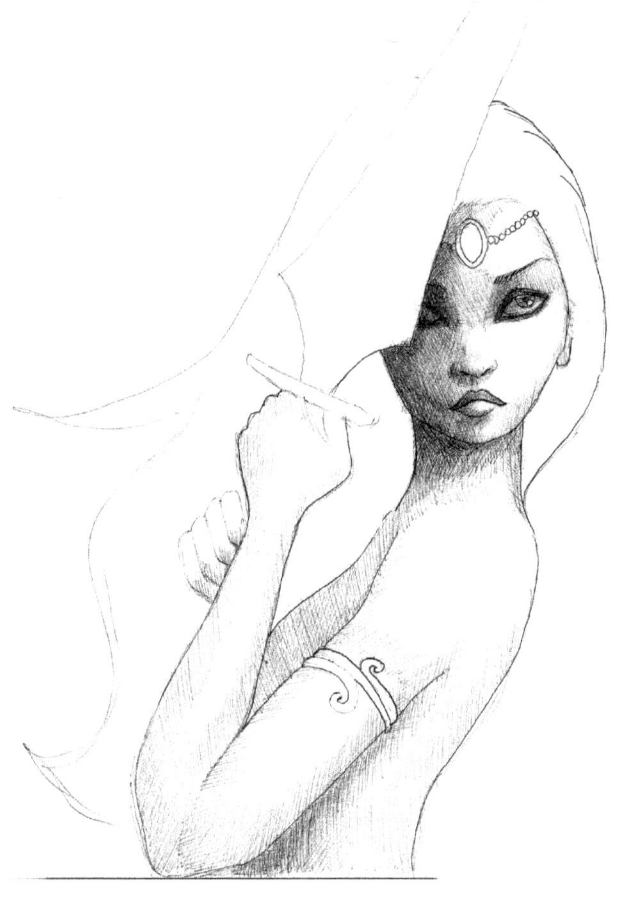

Begin to structure the shaded areas. Define the shading around the eyes and chin areas.

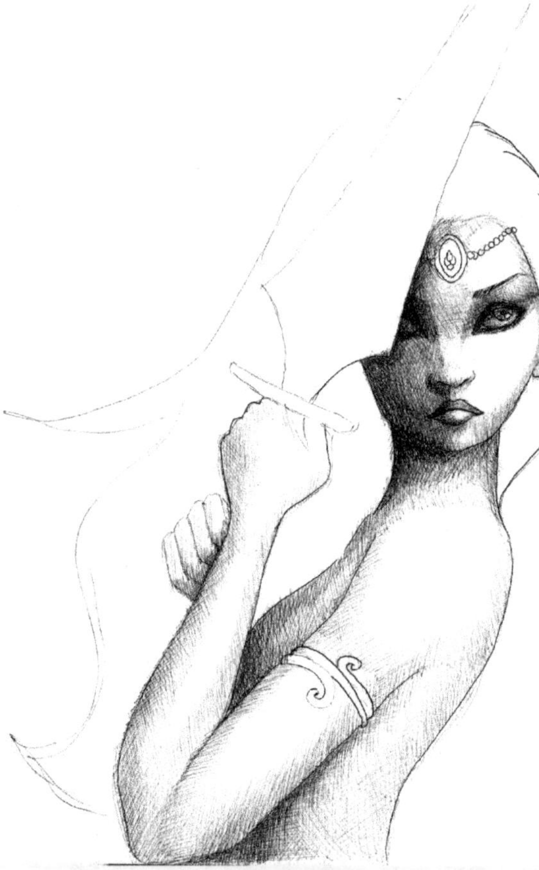

Work on the darker values and areas that transition from dark to light. For example, the shaded area under the chin, and the dark side of her face.

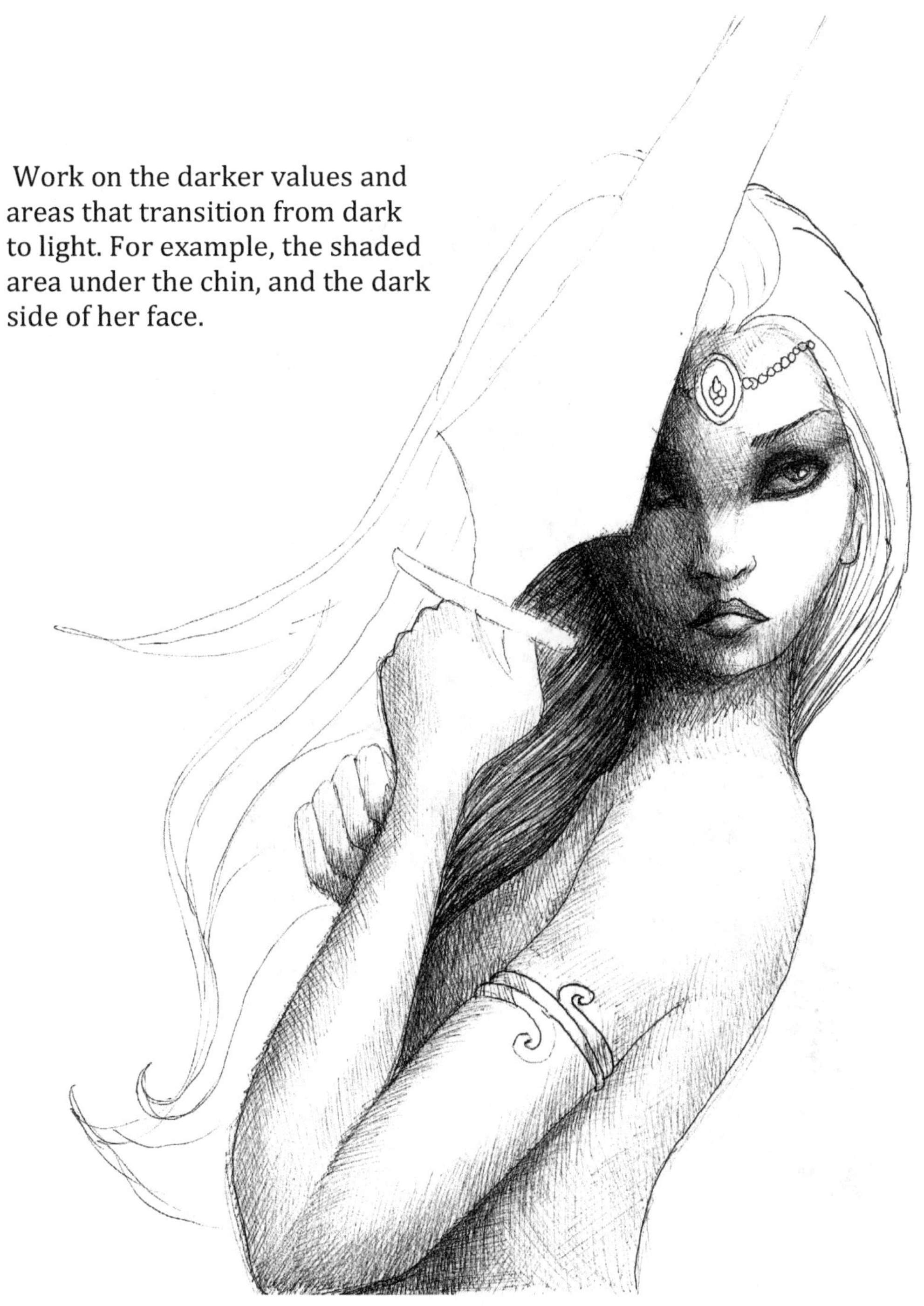

Define and sharpen the face features with the use of your shading.

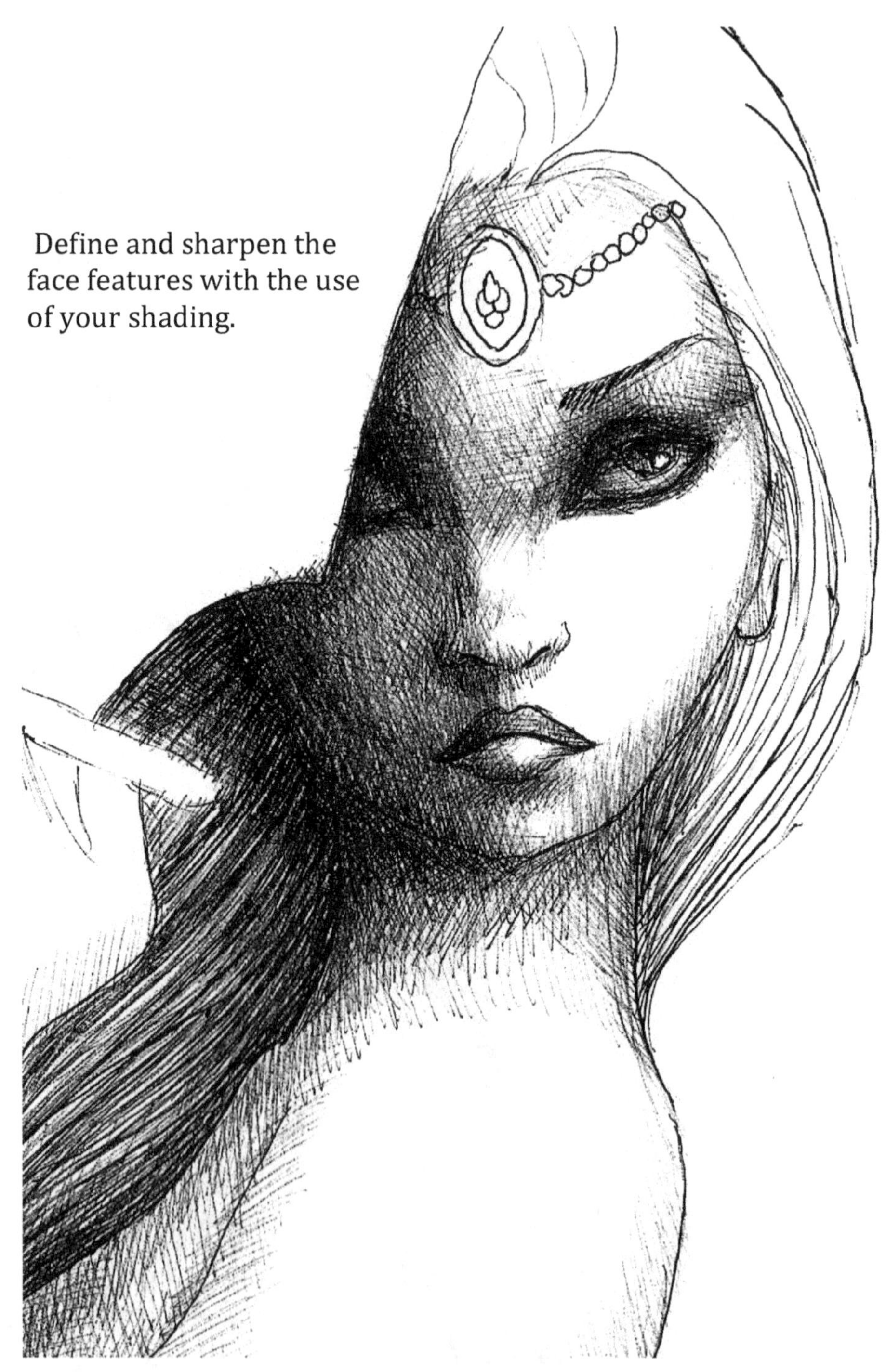

Concentrate on the darkest areas of the shading. Blend the darkest shadows of the face together with the darker parts of the hair.

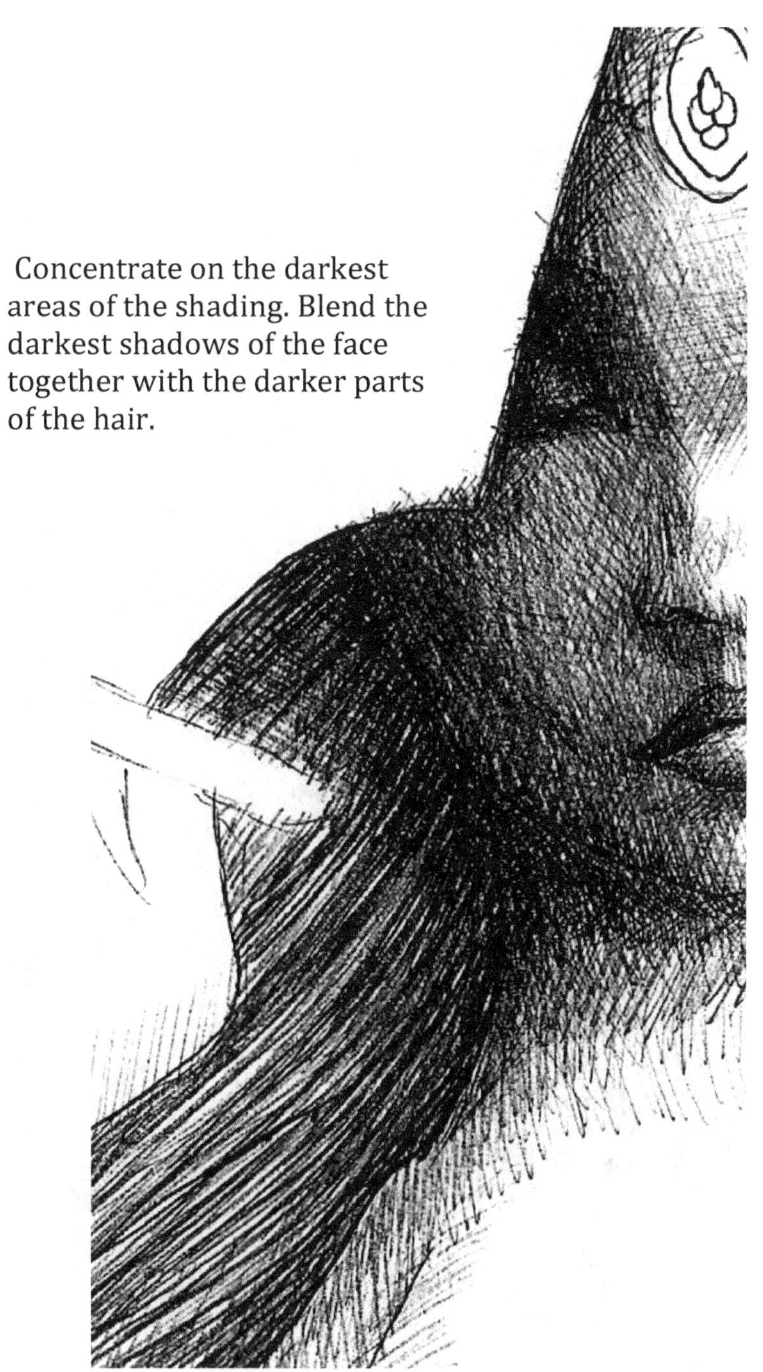

Sit back and examine the overall drawing. Then determine what areas of the shading need more work.

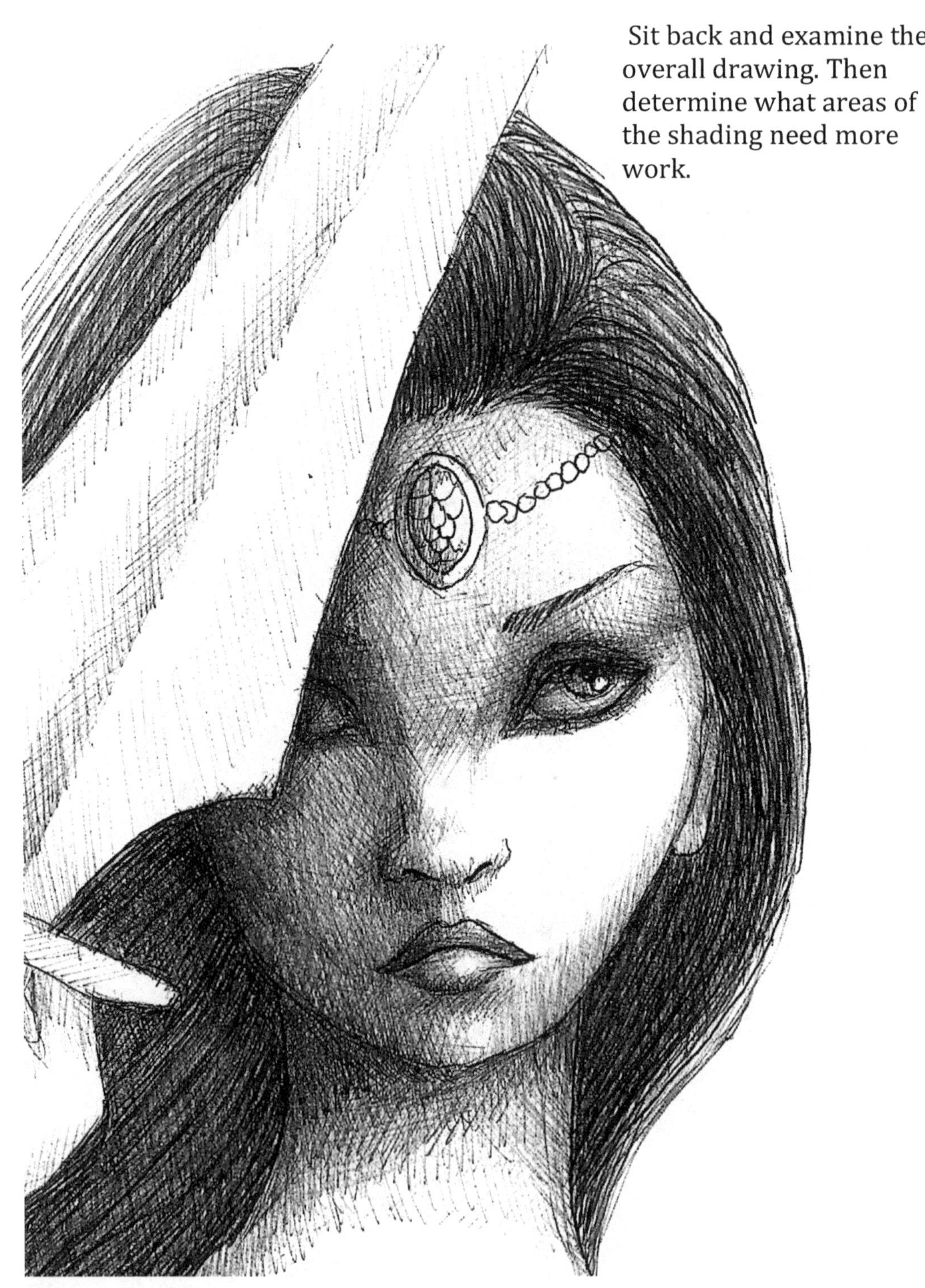

Finish the drawing by doing all the small detail shading. Be meticulous and precise when you get to this point.

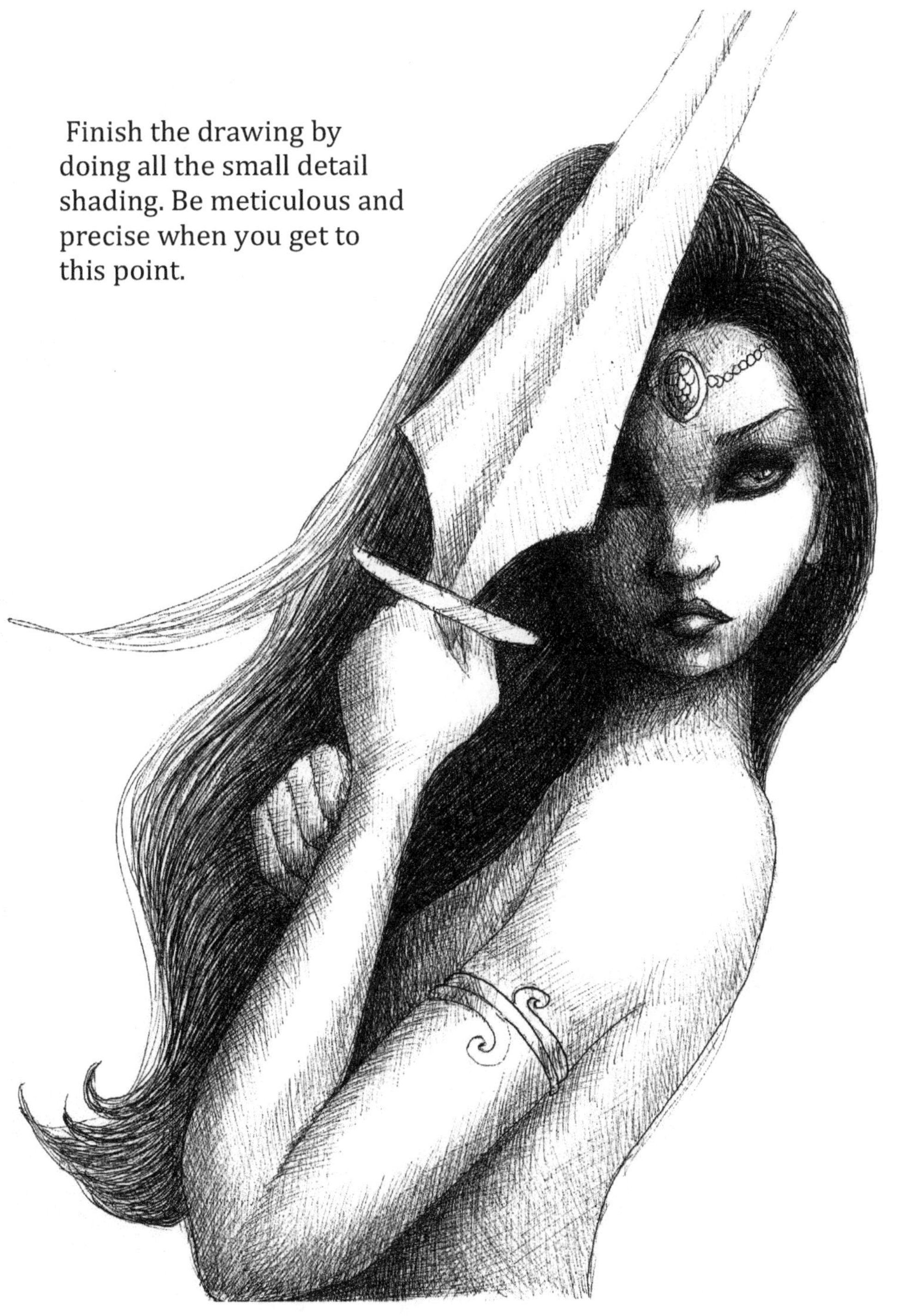

Chapter 6
Conclusion

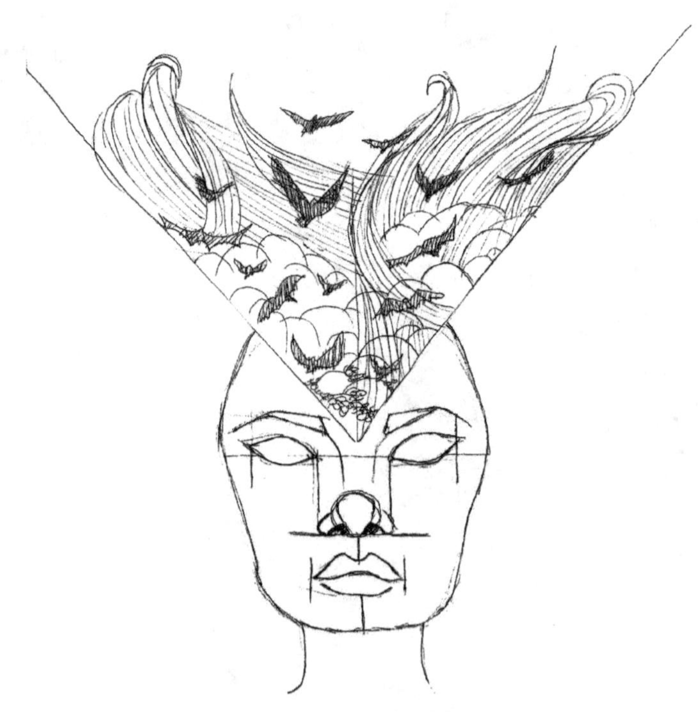

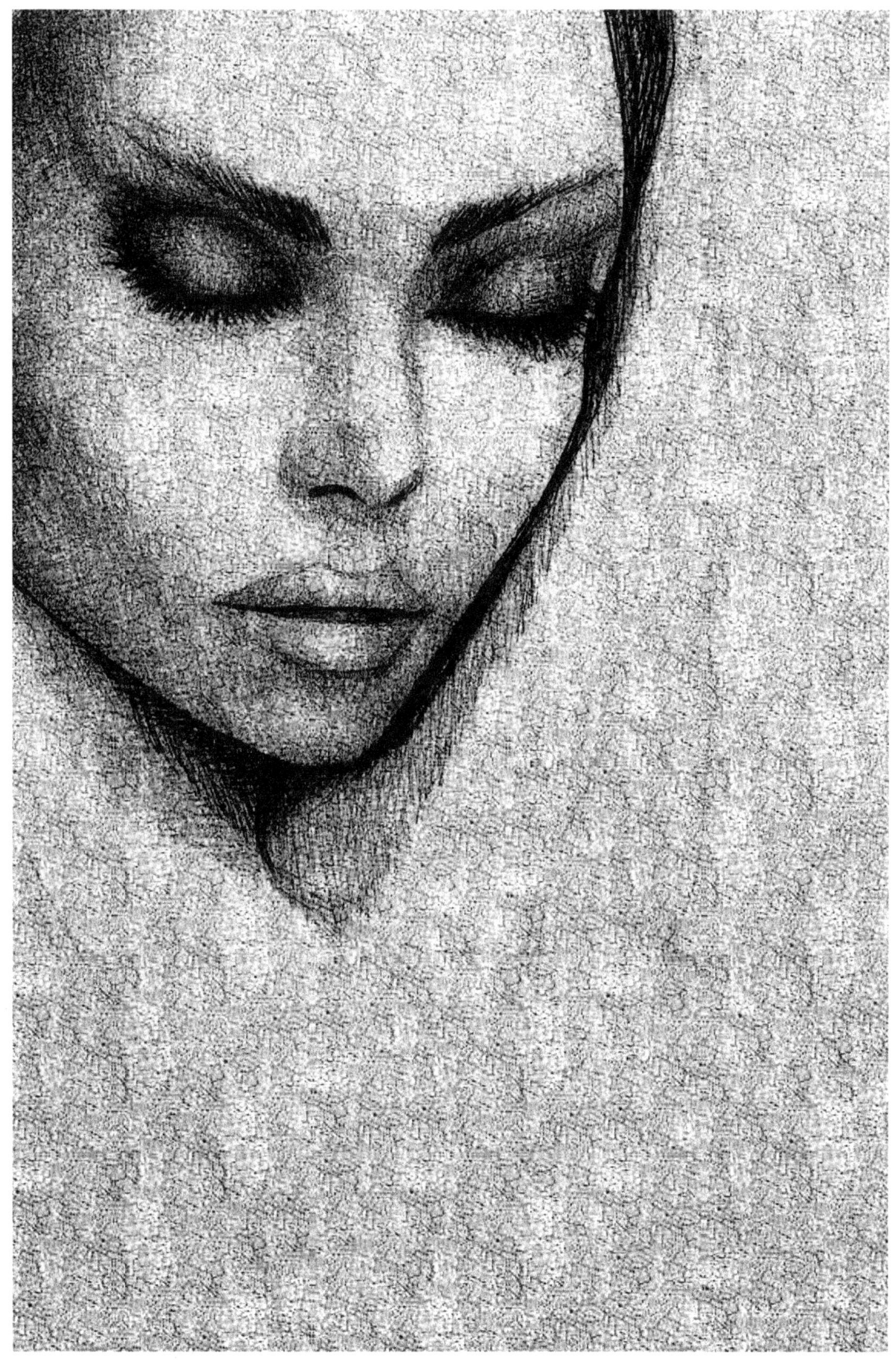

I hope that this book will inspire you to draw and create art on a deep and personal level. It is my hope, that you will exercise the use of your talents every day of your life. In time you will come to the realization that you have been given a precious gift of creative expression and artistic talent.

For it is like the discovery of a hidden garden deep within the confines of your mind. Your talent is a gift that must be appreciated, and cultivated by you. Just like a beautiful garden your talent must be constantly cared for and nurtured. It is a garden that only you can nurture, in order for it to grow and thrive.

Only then will its trees bare the sweetest fruit, and the most rare of roses will bloom. The birds will quench their thirst by the waters of its overflowing fountains of inspiration. Like the birds of this beautiful garden, your talent will soar beyond the confines of your mind.

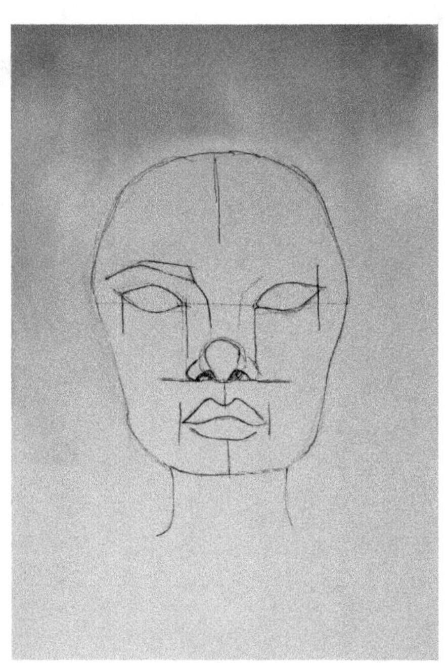

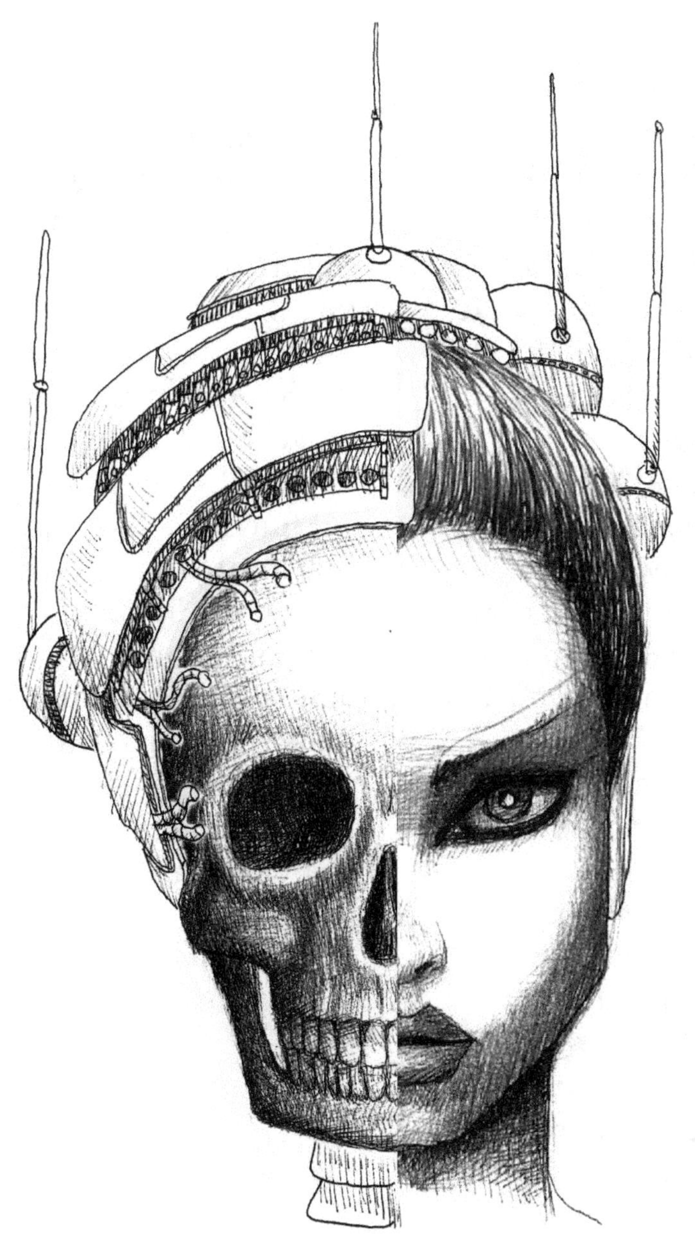

I call this book the lost art of how to draw. Because, it occurred to me that the art of drawing is in danger of being lost. I sometimes wonder if the art of drawing will eventually die out.

With today's technological advances, an artist doesn't even have to know how to draw or paint. Today, an artist can use computer programs for drawing and painting.

For instance, I've seen digital paintings that are better than what many of the old masters could have done. Digital artist are able to produce paintings that rival the masterpieces of Da Vinci, Michelangelo, Rembrandt, Goya, and many more of the great artist in history. I wonder if art historians, in years to come, will consider digital art to be legitimate works of art.

I can only imagine what will be the art of the future. I think of what the art will look like. I imagine what incredible technology artist will have at their fingertips to create it.

I find myself thinking, what art will survive? When the lights of humanity finally flicker and all things beautiful fade into the darkness. In a hundred years or in a thousand years, when the art world grows cold and desolate.

I ask myself what art will endure?

Sometimes I wonder if anyone will look through the worn and tattered pages of our sketchbooks. Will there be anyone to see the faces and the figures that we have drawn.

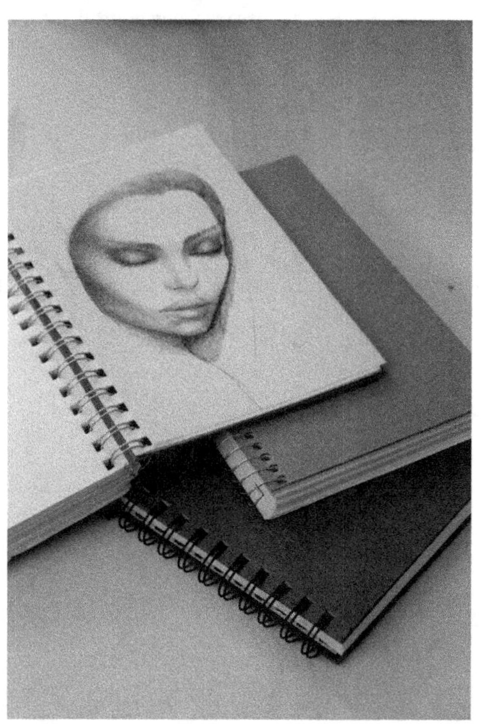

Just like those drawings left behind on the walls of a cold dark cave in Spain. Maybe someday, someone will shine a light and find the sketchbooks we leave behind. The world will know that we existed. They will know that you were an artist, who created art with true and profound passion. And as they turn the pages of your sketchbooks they will see a glimpse of your soul.

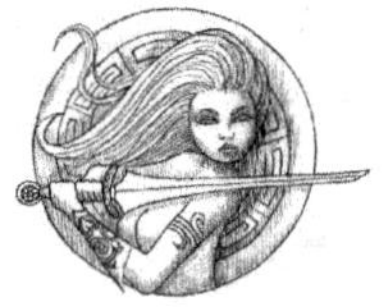

Phoenician Press ©2013

www.ingramcontent.com/pod-product-compliance
Lightning Source LLC
LaVergne TN
LVHW061224100826
845148LV00004B/859

* 9 7 8 0 6 1 5 8 3 5 5 9 4 *